Dublin

Atlantic
Ocean

North
Sea

● Edinburgh

● Belfast

REPUBLIC
OF
IRELAND

GW00707846

HarperCollins*Publishers*

This book was produced using QuarkXPress™ and
Adobe Illustrator 88™ on Apple Macintosh™ computers
and output to separated film on a Linotronic™ 300 Imagesetter

Text: Norman Ross
Photography: James Carney
Cartography: Susan Harvey Design
Design: Kerry Aylin

First published 1991
Copyright © HarperCollins Publishers
Published by HarperCollins Publishers
Produced by Collins Manufacturing, Glasgow
ISBN 0 00 435843 0

HOW TO USE THIS BOOK

Your Collins Traveller Guide will help you find your way around your holiday destination quickly and easily. It is split into two sections which are colour-coded:

The blue section provides you with an alphabetical sequence of headings, from **ART GALLERIES** to **WALKS** via **EXCURSIONS**, **RESTAURANTS**, **SHOPPING**, etc. Each entry within a topic includes information on how to get there, how much it will cost you, when it will be open and what to expect. Furthermore, every page has its own map showing the position of each item and the nearest landmark. This allows you to orientate yourself quickly and easily in your new surroundings.

To find what you want to do – having dinner, visiting a museum, going for a walk or shopping for gifts – simply flick through the blue headings and take your pick!

The red section is an alphabetical list of information. It provides essential facts about places and cultural items – 'What is the Book of Kells?', 'When is Bloomsday?', 'Where is Dun Laoghaire?' – and expands on subjects touched on in the first half of the book. This section also contains practical travel information. It ranges through how to find accommodation, where to hire a car, the variety of eating places and food available, tips on health, information on money, which newspapers are available, how to find a taxi and where the youth hostels are. It is lively and informative and easy to use. Each band shows the first three letters of the first entry on the page. Simply flick through the bands till you find the entry you need!

All the main entries are also cross-referenced to help you find them. Names in small capitals – **MUSEUMS** – tell you that there is more information about the item you are looking for under the topic on museums in the first part of the book. So when you read 'see **MUSEUMS**' you turn to the blue heading for **MUSEUMS**. The instruction 'see **A-Z**', after a word, lets you know that the word has its own entry in the second part of the book. Similarly words in bold type – **Guinness** – also let you know that there is an entry in the A-Z for the indicated name. In both cases you just look under the appropriate heading in the red section. Packed full of information and easy to use – you'll always know where you are with your Collins Traveller Guide!

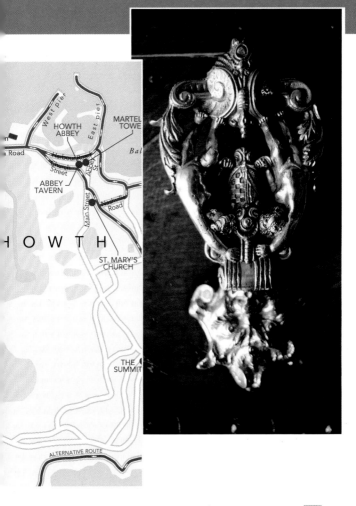

INTRODUCTION

Dublin is a vibrant, thriving, youthful capital, an ancient city more than 1000 years old and a place where one can stay almost a life time yet feel that there is still more to experience. Those who have never been here before may well be surprised by the genuine warmth and good humour of Dubliners, their interest in other people and their capacity for talk – all elements which combine to make visitors to the city feel thoroughly comfortable and at home.

Dublin is, physically, historically and culturally, like the rest of Ireland, heavily influenced by its traditional links with Britain. Despite the Irish establishment's stressing of a new national focus in Europe as part of the EC, Irish culture still fights a constant battle with British influence. But Dublin avoids rationalizing these old links, ignoring them where possible and making the best of them at other times: British newspapers and television are widely available, some of the finest architecture in Europe dates from Dublin's role as the second city of the British Empire, and much of Ireland's 20thC literature is concerned with carving out a new, exclusively Irish identity. The city is famous for its Georgian terraces and for its writers, but its claims to being a 'European cultural centre' or a 'literary city' are more than just an advertising executive's clichés, or the pretensions of the capital of a minor

nation state on the periphery of Europe. In fact, the city exudes scholarship. Its public buildings and universities include some of the finest libraries in the world, while daily lectures at various venues around the city on literary and other cultural topics supplement a roll-call of famous names – from Swift and Burke to Wilde, Shaw, Joyce and Beckett – matched by few other countries, let alone by another city.

Writers, from the newest novelist to newspaper sports columnists, are still stars in the Dublin firmament, and newspaper columns resound to the opinions of commentators, sometimes to the detriment of live news coverage. The provisions of the 1921 Anglo-Irish Treaty or the cult of new Irish writing really can move mere daily party politics off the comment pages in a venting of intellectual spleens which possibly only the French can rival. The city's cultural claims are also supported by the large number of art galleries and cinemas, as well as a thriving theatre – both professional and amateur – with original works by new Irish writers being showcased alongside the classics by the giants of the past like O'Casey and Synge.

But perhaps the enduring symbol of Dublin is its pubs, 800 of them, ranging from classy lounges to smoky beer halls, from Victorian tiled and mirrored palaces to former grocery stores still with original fittings, and from those mentioned in *Ulysses*, novelist James Joyce's classic look at Dublin life, to Edwardian reproductions trying, with varying degrees of success, to evoke the atmosphere experienced by the fictional Leopold Bloom in Joyce's book. Dublin's pubs, the stout and whiskey they serve and the customers who frequent them, are a real-life reflection of this bustling city. They are institutions with their own life style and habits: very few gambling and gaming machines get in the way, for pubs are places to drink and talk, read newspapers, waste time or eat lunch. And you don't have to drink alcohol, as coffee and tea are served everywhere. Pubs are less and less male preserves, with women coming in on their own increasingly, having a drink or something to eat. A typical city pub shows a cross section of Dublin life in the way that a pavement café reflects *la vie Parisienne*.

Like every modern city, Dublin has its bad points: petty crime, heavy traffic, a litter problem, a concrete-jungle mentality among property developers and fast-food commercialism all constantly threaten to scar centuries of history. But few European capitals can match its architectural glories or the many manicured parks and green spaces within the city limits (including more than 20 golf courses and Europe's largest

park) or the sheer vitality of the bustling centre. Even fewer can offer the prospect of staying in a picturesque small fishing town like Howth, yet being just 30 minutes away on a comfortable suburban train from a major European business centre. Or the chance to stand in the middle of the city with a view of a range of mountains which are just an hour's drive away.

Whatever the particular attractions which make you decide to come – be they pubs or parks, museums or mountains, plays or pulpits, shopping or sports – Dublin is a city to be enjoyed at any time of the year.

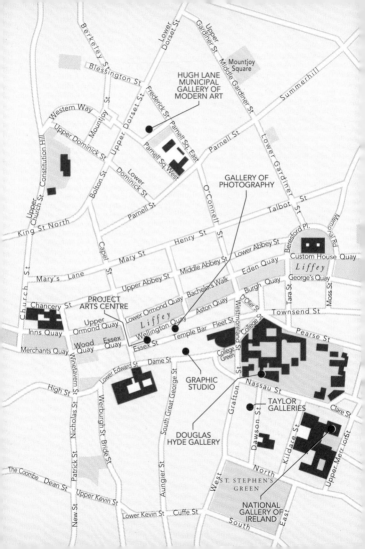

HUGH LANE
MUNICIPAL
GALLERY OF
MODERN ART

GALLERY OF
PHOTOGRAPHY

Custom House Quay

PROJECT
ARTS CENTRE

GRAPHIC
STUDIO

TAYLOR
GALLERIES

DOUGLAS
HYDE GALLERY

NATIONAL
GALLERY OF
IRELAND

Berkeley St
Lower Dorset St
Upper Gardiner St
Middle Gardiner St
Mountjoy Square
Summerhill
Blessington St
Frederick St
Parnell Sq. East
Parnell St
Lower Gardiner St
Western Way
Upper Dominick St
Mountjoy St
Upper Dorset St
Parnell Sq. West
O'Connell St
Talbot St
Constitution Hill
Upper Church St
Lower Dominick St
Bolton St
Parnell St
Beresford Pl.
Memorial Rd
King St North
Mary's Lane
Capel St
Mary St
Henry St
Lower Abbey St
Eden Quay
George's Quay
Moss St
Liffey
Chancery St
Upper Abbey St
Middle Abbey St
Bachelor's Walk
Burgh Quay
Tara St
Church St
Inns Quay
Upper Ormond Quay
Lower Ormond Quay
Wellington Quay
Aston Quay
D'Olier St
Westmoreland St
Townsend St
Merchants Quay
Wood Quay
Essex Quay
Essex St
Temple Bar
Fleet St
College St
Pearse St
Wineavern St
Lower Edward St
Dame St
College Green
Nassau St
High St
Patrick St
Nicholas St
Werburgh St
Bride St
South Great George St
Aungier St
Grafton St
Dawson St
Kildare St
Clare St
Upper Merrion St
The Coombe
Dean St
Upper Kevin St
Lower Kevin St
Cuffe St
New St
West
St. Stephen's Green
North
South
East

NATIONAL GALLERY OF IRELAND Merrion Sq., tel: 615133.
❑ 1000-1800 Mon.-Wed., Fri., Sat., 1000-2100 Thu., 1400-1700 Sun.
Sun. tours 1430, 1500, 1530, 1600, lecture 1500. DART Pearse Station.
*Opened in 1864 and now showing over 2000 pictures from all European
schools, including works by Goya, Poussin and Gainsborough and by
Irish painters Ashford, Barrett, Yeats, Hone, Osborne, Lavery and Orpen.*

HUGH LANE MUNICIPAL GALLERY OF MODERN ART
Charlemont House, Parnell Sq., tel: 741903. ❑ 0930-1800 Tue.-Sat.,
1100-1700 Sun. DART Tara St, Connolly Station.
*Hugh Lane's outstanding collection of 19th-20thC paintings, split in two
and shared with London's National Gallery, is changed every five years.*

DOUGLAS HYDE GALLERY Trinity College (Nassau St entrance),
College Green, tel: 772941 ext. 1116. ❑ 1100-1800 Mon.-Wed., Fri.,
1100-1900 Thu., 1100-1645 Sat. DART Tara St.
*Enjoys a reputation for staging good exhibitions by Irish and foreign con-
temporary painters and sculptors. Works are not for sale.*

GALLERY OF PHOTOGRAPHY 35 Wellington Quay, tel: 714654.
❑ 1100-1800 Mon.-Sat., 1200-1800 Sun. DART Tara St.
*Ireland's top photography gallery. Changing exhibitions of works, many
for sale, by leading photographers from home and abroad.*

GRAPHIC STUDIO 8 Cope St, tel: 6798021.
❑ 1030-1800 Mon.-Sat. DART Tara St.
Exhibitions of etchings, blocks and screenprints by Irish graphic artists.

PROJECT ARTS CENTRE 39 Essex St East, tel: 712321.
❑ 1130-2000 Mon.-Sat. DART Tara St.
This multi-arts centre is a good place to see and buy avant-garde works.

TAYLOR GALLERIES 6 Dawson St, tel: 776089.
DART Tara St, Pearse Station. ❑ 1000-1730 Mon.-Fri., 1100-1300 Sat.
*Gallery with a long-standing reputation for quality exhibitions of works
by leading Irish artists such as Anne Madden and Patrick Scott.*

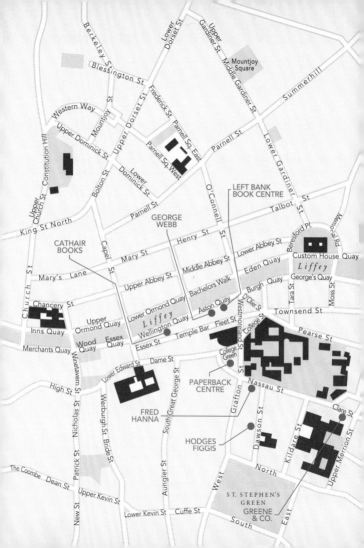

CATHAIR BOOKS 1 Essex Gate, tel: 6792406.
❏ 1000-1800 Mon.-Sat. DART Tara St.
Antiquarian and second-hand bookshop hidden in an alley behind Dame St. It carries a good selection of English- and Irish-language titles, including leather-bound editions.

HODGES FIGGIS 41 Dawson St, tel: 774754.
❏ 0900-1830 Mon.-Sat., 1100-1800 Sun. DART Tara St, Pearse Station.
There is a wide range of titles in this pleasant, two-storey shop. Known for its selection of Irish history, Irish fiction and Irish-language books.

FRED HANNA 27/29 Nassau St, tel: 771255.
❏ 0900-1730 Mon.-Sat. DART Tara St, Pearse Station.
*General university bookshop carrying academic and lighter titles. Enjoys a big trade with students from Trinity College (see **A-Z**) opposite.*

GREENE & CO. 16 Clare St, tel: 762554.
❏ 0900-1730 Mon.-Sat. DART Pearse Station.
A famous name catering for university students and general readers, with mainly academic new and second-hand books.

PAPERBACK CENTRE 20 Suffolk St, tel: 774210.
❏ 0930-1800 Mon.-Wed., Sat., 0930-2100 Thu., Fri. DART Tara St.
A good selection of paperback titles from Ireland and elsewhere can be found in this shop which stands in an alley behind Grafton St.

GEORGE WEBB 5 Crampton Quay, tel: 777489.
❏ 0900-1930 Mon.-Sat. DART Tara St.
*A browser's delight located near the Halfpenny Bridge (see **A-Z**). Famous for its pavement trays of bargains. Inside are new and second-hand books of Irish interest.*

LEFT BANK BOOK CENTRE 4 Crampton Quay, tel: 6798348.
❏ 0900-1730 Mon.-Sat. DART Tara St.
Small, friendly shop specializing in political and feminist titles but with something for everyone. Not exclusively 20thC material; includes fiction.

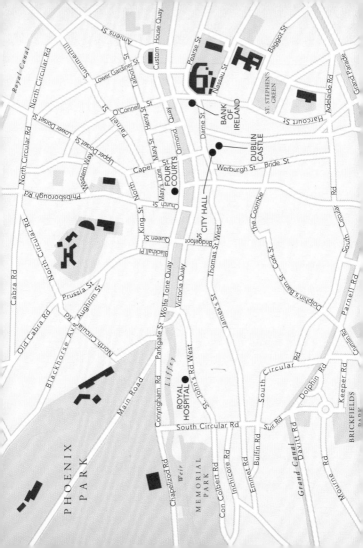

BANK OF IRELAND College Green, tel: 615933.
❑ 1000-1230 Mon.-Fri., 1330-1500 Mon.-Wed., Fri., 1300-1700 Thu.
Entry to former House of Lords by arrangement. DART Tara St. ❑ Free.
*Grand, windowless home of Irish Parliament until the 1800 union with
Britain. Treasures include Commons' mace and 1735 tapestries of Battle
of Boyne and Siege of Derry. Portico statues represent Hibernia, Fortitude,
Fidelity, Commerce, Justice, Liberty. Commons' chamber is now an office.*

CITY HALL Lord Edward St, tel: 6796111.
❑ 0900-1300, 1415-1700 Mon.-Fri. DART Tara St. ❑ Free.
*Built (1769-79) as the Royal Exchange, this is now the headquarters of
Dublin corporation. Houses 102 Royal Charters and the mace and sword
of the city, all on display with statues of Irish notables. Its fine coffered
dome is best viewed from inside the circular central hall. See* **WALK 1**.

DUBLIN CASTLE Dame St, tel: 777580/777129.
❑ 1000-1215, 1400-1700 Mon.-Fri., 1400-1700 Sat.-Sun. Closes for
state occasions. DART Tara St. ❑ £1, 50p child, senior citizen.
*Architectural, historical and artistic treasure house dating from 13th-
19thC. See the State Apartments, including the high, panelled ceiling in
St. Patrick's Hall, and Church of the Most Holy Trinity. See* **WALK 1**, **A-Z**.

FOUR COURTS Inns Quay, tel: 725555.
❑ 1100-1300, 1400-1600 Mon.-Fri. DART Tara St. ❑ Free.
*Grand Georgian courts (1802) by architect James Gandon. The 100-yard
frontage has a mixture of triumphal arches, courtyards, colonnades and a
green copper central dome which dominates the quayside skyline. It was
damaged by shelling in the Civil War (see* **Ireland***) and reopened in
1931. Visitors can see Supreme and High Courts in action. See* **WALK 1**.

ROYAL HOSPITAL St. John's Rd, Kilmainham, tel: 718666.
❑ 1200-1700 Tue.-Sun. Bus 68, 69 from Fleet St; 79 from Aston Quay.
❑ Free Tue.; £1 Wed.-Fri., £1.50 Sat., Sun. Senior citizens free.
*Modelled on Les Invalides and built by William Robinson for Charles II's
old soldiers. Beautiful interior and chapel with a fine stucco ceiling. Now
renovated as arts centre with concerts, exhibitions and open-air theatre.*

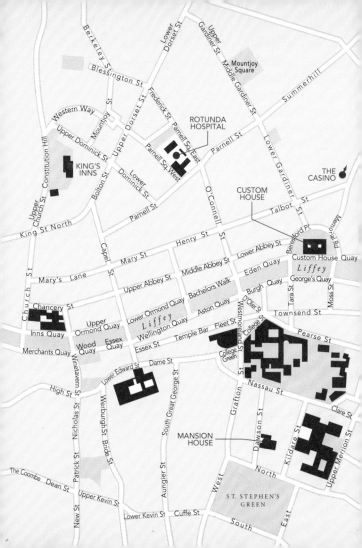

ROTUNDA HOSPITAL Parnell Sq., tel: 730700.
❑ Normal working hours Mon.-Fri. Visits to chapel by appointment.
DART Connolly Station.
*Founded by Dr Bartholomew Mosse and built by Richard Cassels (1750),
this was the first purpose-built maternity hospital in the British Isles and
it is still a working hospital. Rotunda Hall, built in 1755 by George Ensor,
is now a cinema, while the Rotunda Chapel is famous for its plasterwork
(by Bartholomew Cramillion, 1758).*

KING'S INNS Constitution Hill and Henrietta St, tel: 747134.
❑ Park open to the public; access to main building and library only if
accompanied by a member. Bus 34/A from Middle Abbey St.
*Superb James Gandon building (1795-1817), now a base for barristers;
its library has 100,000 volumes. A courtyard links the park and Henrietta
St (now run down but with fine early-Georgian houses; see* **Architecture***).*

CUSTOM HOUSE Custom House Quay, tel: 363122.
❑ Not open to the public. DART Tara St.
*Beautiful Georgian building (1781-91) by James Gandon dominates the
lower Liffey quays. Arcade, friezes, statues and arches of Portland stone
and granite are topped by a graceful, green copper dome. The building
was reduced to a shell by fire in 1921 but was restored.*

MANSION HOUSE Dawson St, tel: 761337.
❑ By appointment. DART Tara St, Pearse Station.
*The Lord Mayor's official residence is a Queen Anne brick building
(1710) by Joseph Dawson, after whom the street on which it stands is
named. Scene of the Declaration of Independence in 1919. See* **WALK 1***.*

THE CASINO Marino, Malahide Rd, tel: 331618.
❑ 1000-1900 May-Sep.; 1000-1600 Sat., 1400-1600 Sun. (Oct.-April).
Bus 27/A from Lower Gardiner St, 27B from Beresford Place, 42/A/B/C,
43 from Talbot St.
*Lord Charlemont's superb Palladian-style 'weekend cottage' (by William
Chambers, 1758), with ornate fireplaces and period furniture. Dracula
author Bram Stoker was born in 15 Marino Crescent half a mile south.*

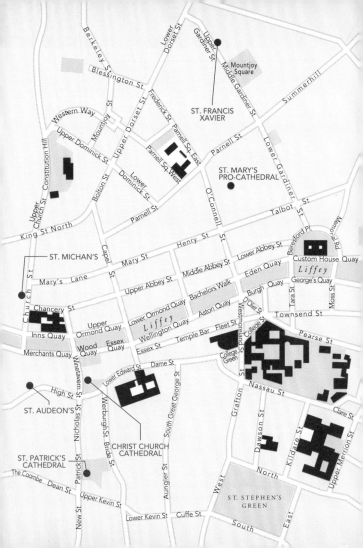

Catholic churches (c) usually open throughout the day, Anglican Church of Ireland (a) usually closed except for services and specific times.

CHRIST CHURCH CATHEDRAL (a), Christ Church Place, tel: 778099. ❏ 1000-1700 Mon.-Sat. (May-Sep.), 0930-1245, 1430-1700 Tue.-Fri., 0930-1245 Sat. (Oct.-April). DART Tara St. ❏ Donation.
Founded in 1038 by Norse King Sitric, rebuilt by Normans and restored last century. Contains the tomb of Strongbow (see A-Z) and memorials to British rule over Ireland. Musty crypt makes an eerie visit. See WALK 1.

ST. PATRICK'S CATHEDRAL (a), Patrick St, tel: 754817.
❏ 0830-1815 Mon.-Fri., 0830-1700 Sat., 0830-0900, 1000-1630 Sun. Bus 21A, 78A/B from Fleet St. DART Tara St. ❏ Admission charge.
Majestic 13thC cathedral on oldest Christian site in Dublin, dating from 5thC (see St. Patrick). Satirist Jonathan Swift (see A-Z) is buried here.

ST. FRANCIS XAVIER (c), Upper Gardiner St, tel: 363411.
❏ Service times. DART Connolly Station.
One of the city's finest churches, by J. B. Keane (1832). Italian marble altarpiece, richly decorated with lapis lazuli; splendid coffered ceiling.

ST. MARY'S PRO-CATHEDRAL (c), Marlborough St, tel: 745441. DART Tara St, Connolly Station.
This grand building's Athenian temple facade looks spectacularly out of place among the backstreets. By an amateur architect, it has a beautiful Renaissance interior and dome based on St.-Phillippe de Reule in Paris.

ST. AUDEON'S (a), High St, tel: 6797099.
❏ 1000-1630 Tue.-Sat. DART Tara St.
The city's oldest parish church, built in 12thC. Its tower has three bells cast in 1423, and St. Audeon's Arch was part of the original city walls.

ST. MICHAN'S (a), Church St, tel: 724154.
❏ 1000-1245 Mon.-Sat., 1400-1645 Mon.-Fri. DART Tara St.
Founded in 1095 by the Danes and famous for the mummified medieval bodies in its vaults. Handel played Messiah on the organ here.

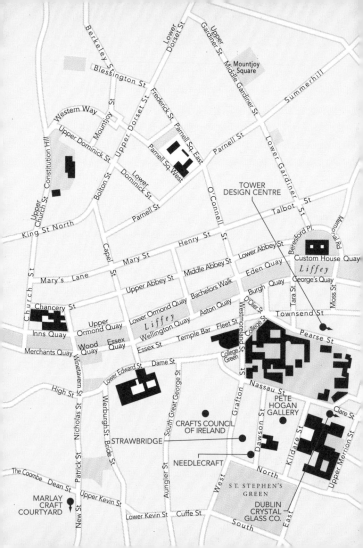

CRAFTS COUNCIL OF IRELAND Powerscourt Town House, Clarendon St, tel: 6797368. ❏ See **Opening Times**. DART Tara St.
Clearing house for information about all Irish arts and crafts. Examples often for sale, especially at popular Christmas and summer exhibitions.

DUBLIN CRYSTAL GLASS CO. Brookfield Terrace, Carysfort Ave, Blackrock, tel: 887932/888627. ❏ 0900-1730 Mon.-Fri., 1000-1300 Sat. Closed part of Aug. Bus 7A from Eden Quay, 45 from Burgh Quay. DART Blackrock.
Crystal cutting and engraving factory. See the cutters at work through a window in the showroom. Reduced prices for factory produce.

MARLAY CRAFT COURTYARD Marlay Park, Rathfarnham, tel: 942083. ❏ Shop 1100-1730 Mon.-Sat., 1400-1730 Sun.
Bus 47B, 48A from Hawkins St.
*Watch the craftspeople in their workshops: bookbinders, clockmakers, glass-blowers, copperworkers, harp makers, etc. See **PARKS & GARDENS**.*

NEEDLECRAFT 27 Dawson St, tel: 772493.
❏ See **Opening Times**. DART Tara St, Pearse Station.
Everything for needlepoint and cross-stitch; designer knitting and tapestry, including original Irish needlepoint designs; Aran sweater patterns.

PETE HOGAN GALLERY 38 Molesworth St, tel: 765288, or tel: 282630 for appointment. ❏ 1030-1730 Mon.-Fri. DART Pearse Station.
Dublin and Irish scenes by a well-known artist. Commissions accepted.

STRAWBRIDGE 8 Lemon St, tel: 6798603.
❏ 1000-1730 Mon.-Sat. DART Tara St, Pearse Station.
High-quality traditional furniture, including free standing kitchen units and dressers, made to order in Irish wood. No shipping service.

TOWER DESIGN CENTRE Pearse St, tel: 775655.
❏ 0900-1715 Mon.-Fri., 1000-1300 Sat. DART Pearse Station.
Ireland's largest arts and crafts centre, with 35 businesses selling stained glass, wood carvings, woven goods, hand-knits, ceramics and more. Café.

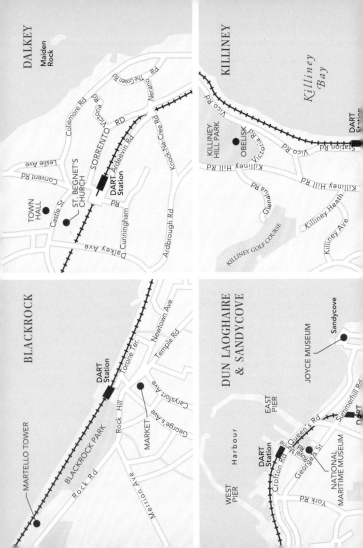

*A day out on the DART (see **A-Z**), from Blackrock to Killiney, taking in the coastal towns of Dun Laoghaire (see **A-Z**), Sandycove and Dalkey (see **A-Z**).*

Start from Tara St station in the city centre and take the southbound train for Bray. The line goes past Lansdowne Rd, dominated by the stadium where Ireland play international soccer and rugby matches (see **Sports**), through the fashionable residential areas of Ballsbridge and Sandymount, before joining the Dublin Bay coastline at Merrion Strand. The train passes through Booterstown before your first stop, Blackrock, a seaside suburb best known for its rugby club which has produced generations of Irish internationalists, and for Blackrock College public school where, among others, rock singer and philanthropist Bob Geldof was a pupil. Alongside the DART station is small but pretty Blackrock Park, with a Martello tower (see **A-Z**) at its northeastern end. The shore on either side of the station has bathing places. A good craft and flea market takes place in Blackrock at weekends (see **MARKETS**).

Back on the DART for three stops, you then reach Dun Laoghaire, a grand Victorian port 6.5 miles from Dublin, still stately although with a slightly shabby air (see **Walks**). Stroll along its massive granite piers, each over a mile long. The view from east pier is best. The National Maritime Museum is in a converted church in nearby Haigh Terrace, tel: 800969 (1430-1730 Tue.-Sun., May-Sep.; 1430-1730 Sat., Sun., April, Oct., Nov.). Among its fascinating exhibits is a French longboat captured at Bantry, Co. Cork, in 1796.

Next stop is Sandycove, a seaside village now absorbed into the Dublin-Dun Laoghaire-Bray suburban sprawl. It is probably best known as the starting point for Leopold Bloom's odyssey around Dublin on 16 June 1904, recorded in *Ulysses* (see **Bloomsday**). The Martello tower (built in 1804; see **A-Z**) on Harbour Rd (just over a mile from DART station) houses the Joyce Museum (1000-1300, 1400-1700 Mon.-Sat., 1430-1800 Sun., April-Oct. £1.30, children 70p).

Resume your journey for two stops to alight at Dalkey, a Georgian and Victorian seaside town with many well-preserved period houses and cottages, particularly on Sorrento Rd which runs down from the railway

station (see **Walks**). The town's old-world atmosphere is enhanced by Archbold's Castle, the 16thC town hall, St. Begnet's Church and various pubs with their 19thC wood panelling and brass in pristine condition. Summer boat trips are available to Dalkey Island.

One more stop will take you to Killiney where the station is set down by the coastline, with woods and housing all around (see **Walks**). Head north from the station onto Vico Rd, which has panoramic views of Bray, the Wicklow Mountains and Killiney Bay. The bay itself has been likened to the Bay of Naples, and many of the houses around the bay have Italian names. Join Killiney Hill Rd by going left up Victoria Rd to reach Killiney Hill Park, originally part of Killiney Castle estate. A 1.5-mile walk will take you to the top of the hill which is dominated by an 18thC obelisk, built to provide work for local workers during a period of unemployment.

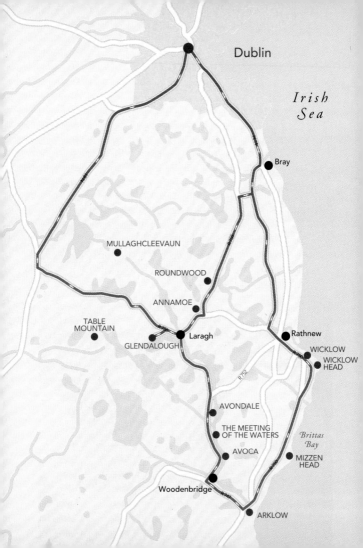

A one-day excursion south through Co. Wicklow, visiting Arklow, the Vale of Avoca, Avondale and Glendalough.

Head out of the city centre on Merrion Rd for Dun Laoghaire and then follow the N 11 through the coastal towns and villages like Dalkey and Bray, which grew up independently but which are now part of suburban Dublin. After 30 miles, at Rathnew, turn left for Wicklow town. Take the coast road out of Wicklow, hugging the cliffs and sand dunes of Wicklow Head, Brittas Bay and Mizzen Head before reaching Arklow. This road from Wicklow to Arklow is a designated scenic route of beautiful wild countryside and is lined with picture-postcard cottages.

Arklow is a port famous for its centuries-old trade of shipbuilding: *Gipsy Moth IV*, the yacht in which Sir Francis Chichester sailed solo around the world, was built here. The Catholic Wexford rebellion of 1798 led by Fr John Murphy also ended here. Apart from its boats, Arklow is now best known for Arklow Pottery, Japanese-owned but Irish-made.

Take the R 747 to Woodenbridge and then turn right onto the R 752 for the Vale of Avoca. The town of Avoca, set by the river, is known for its craftwork by Avoca Handweavers, where capes, ponchos, bedspreads and scarves are made. Along the whole road from here to Glendalough are a number of craft shops selling jewellery, hand-knits and so on. The rivers Avonbeg and Avonmore meet to form the River Avoca (known locally as 'The Meeting of the Waters') about 1.5 miles to the north of Avoca. National poet Tom Moore wrote that the area was 'a valley so sweet', and his words are still true today. At the confluence is The Meetings, a pub with a restaurant and craft shop built on the site of the cottage where Moore lived.

Return to the road and, 2 miles further on, turn off it to the right to arrive at Avondale, beautiful country home of 19thC nationalist leader Charles Stewart Parnell (see **A-Z**). Built in 1777 and now occupied by the Forestry Service, the 530-acre estate and house can both be visited. Return to the main road, which follows the Vale of Clara, another beautiful wooded valley, until you reach Laragh; veer left onto the R 756 and you will soon see signs to the left indicating Glendalough.

The road up to the monastic settlement is about 1.25 miles long and is busy with pedestrians in summer and at weekends, so drive carefully. Parking is plentiful and free at the settlement's visitor centre which has a superb audio-visual presentation and small display area.

Glendalough (the Valley of the Two Lakes) was a religious site for 12 centuries and was the most important ecclesiastical centre in Wicklow, at a time when the Celtic Church in Ireland was the main centre for Christian scholarship. It is now a major tourist attraction. Conservation work on its buildings started as early as 1873 and has continued since. Fed by the River Poulnass, its lakes were the site of a hermitage established by St. Kevin (d. 619) after finishing his monastic training at Kilnamanagh, near Tallaght, south Dublin. Kevin had a reputation for saintliness and Glendalough became a notable place of pilgrimage until it was suppressed by Cardinal Cullen of Dublin in 1862. The 103-ft-high Norman Round Tower dominates the south of the main

lake where the monastic community flourished for so long. 150 yards away to the southwest is St. Mary's Church, which might have belonged to a convent of nuns, while southeast is St. Peter's and St. Paul's Cathedral, with 10thC nave and 12thC chancel and sacristy. Southwest of the cathedral is a monastic cemetery with a priest's house at the centre, dating from the 12thC. Other churches and religious buildings scattered all around the site include the small St. Kevin's Church which, even though just a little room amid a ruin, served as the local Catholic church from 1810-50.

You have a choice of route after leaving the car park: you can re-trace your steps south to Laragh and follow the scenic R 755 through picturesque villages like Annamoe and Roundwood before turning right back onto the N 11 for Dublin, near Bray.

Alternatively, if the weather is fine when you leave Glendalough, you may choose to take the northernmost fork in the road (R 756) outside the car park and drive over the mountains through the beautiful Wicklow Gap into Co. Kildare. On your right is Mullaghcleevaun, while the peak on your left is Table Mountain.

Return to Dublin by the N 81.

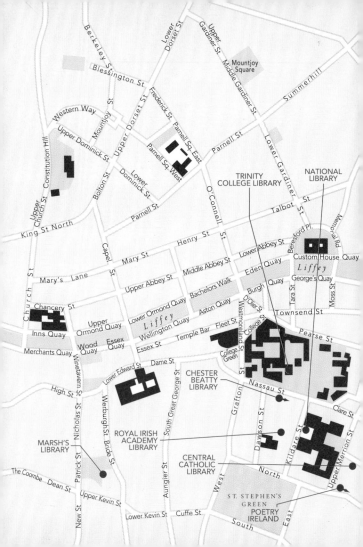

TRINITY COLLEGE LIBRARY College Green, tel: 772941.
❑ 0930-1645 Mon.-Fri., 0930-1245 Sat., Sun. DART Tara St. ❑ £1.75.
The Long Room (by Thomas Burgh, 1712) was Europe's biggest reading room when built. Among the treasures is the magnificent Book of Kells (see A-Z). Historical exhibitions are held in central aisle. See A-Z.

MARSH'S LIBRARY St. Patrick's Close, tel: 543511.
❑ 1000-1245, 1400-1700 Mon., Wed.-Fri., 1030-1230 Sat. DART Tara St.
Archbishop Marsh's collection is Ireland's oldest public library (1701). See the cages into which readers were locked to prevent theft of books.

NATIONAL LIBRARY Kildare St, tel: 618811.
❑ 1000-2100 Mon.-Thu., 1000-1700 Fri., 1000-1300 Sat. DART Pearse S.
*Over 500,000 books, Irish maps, manuscripts, newspapers and magazines. Helpful staff, especially for ancestor-researchers (see **Genealogy**).*

POETRY IRELAND 44 Upper Mount St, tel: 610320.
❑ 1400-1700 Mon.-Fri. DART Pearse Station.
96,000 volumes, mostly of Irish poetry, collected by poet Austin Clarke, including many now out of print. Meeting place for writers. Readings.

ROYAL IRISH ACADEMY LIBRARY 19 Dawson St, tel: 762570.
❑ 0930-2200 Mon., 0930-1730 Tue.-Fri. DART Tara St, Pearse Station.
Extensive collection of ancient Irish manuscripts, including many written on vellum, from the pre- and early-Christian period.

CENTRAL CATHOLIC LIBRARY 74 Merrion Sq., tel: 761264.
❑ 1100-1930 Mon.-Sat. DART Pearse Station.
Unusual selection of Irish and foreign Catholic periodicals and newspapers dating back decades. 80,000 books on general and religious topics.

CHESTER BEATTY LIBRARY 20 Shrewsbury Rd, tel: 692386.
❑ 1000-1700 Tue.-Fri., 1400-1700 Sat. Free tours 1430 Wed., Sat.
Bus 46, 84 from College St. DART Sandymount, Sydney Parade.
This bequest is one of the finest private collections of Islamic and oriental manuscripts, with a Babylonian clay tablet from 2700 BC.

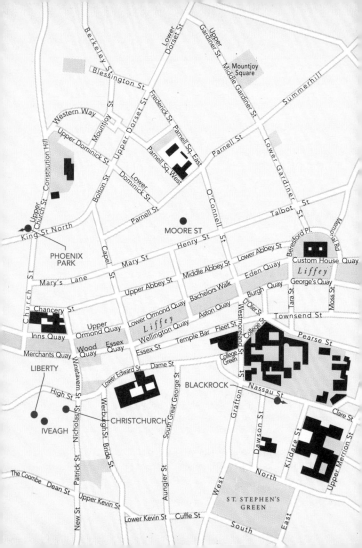

BLACKROCK 19a Main St, Blackrock.
❑ 1100-1730 Sat., 1200-1730 Sun. Bus 7/A, 8 from Eden Quay.
DART Blackrock.
A combination of flea market and craft show. Antiques, hand-knitted woollens, handmade furniture, bric-a-brac and books all sold in a converted old home. Busy and worth a look. See **EXCURSION 1**.

CHRISTCHURCH Back Lane, High St.
❑ 1000-1700. Bus 21A, 78A/B from Fleet St. DART Tara St.
Arts and crafts market located behind Tailors' Hall (1707) the city's oldest surviving guildhall, and selling everything from silver and jewellery to leather goods, furniture, linens and touristy craft pieces.

MOORE ST West of O'Connell St.
❑ 0900-1800 Mon.-Sat. DART Tara St, Connolly Station.
Dublin's best-known market, where the banter between stallholders and customers makes for a lively atmosphere. Mainly meat and vegetable stalls, flower sellers and some of the best-priced produce you can find.

IVEAGH Francis St.
❑ 0900-1800 Tue.-Sat. Bus 21A, 78A/B from Fleet St. DART Tara St.
Flea market set in the old Liberties district of the city, close to Liberty (see below). Its main trade is in second-hand clothes. Popular with the trendy student set, although anyone can pick up a bargain here.

LIBERTY Meath St.
❑ 1000-1800 Fri., Sat. Bus 21A, 78A/B from Fleet St. DART Tara St.
Also set in the Liberties, just a block from the Iveagh (see above). A sprawling market where the visitor can join Dubliners shopping for new and second-hand clothes and household goods.

PHOENIX PARK Racecourse, Castleknock.
❑ 1400-1800 Sun. Bus 8A/C from Middle Abbey St; 70, 80 from Lower Ormond Quay.
Basically a large car-boot sale, with everything from clothing and crafts to household goods and home-made products.

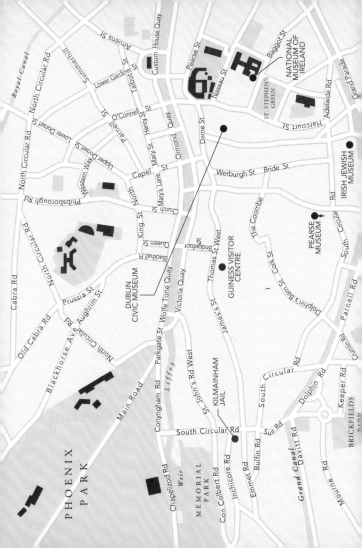

NATIONAL MUSEUM OF IRELAND Kildare St, tel: 765521.
❏ 1000-1700 Tue.-Sat., 1400-1700 Sun. DART Pearse Station. ❏ Free.
A panorama of Irish history. Bronze Age artefacts, including woven-gold jewellery, are impressive, as are early-Christian pieces. See **A-Z***.*

DUBLIN CIVIC MUSEUM 58 William St South, tel: 6794260.
❏ 1000-1800 Tue.-Sat., 1100-1400 Sun. DART Tara St. ❏ Free.
Newspapers, posters, maps, prints and other artefacts depict city history from Stone Age times. Among the exhibits is Nelson's head from Nelson's Pillar (formerly in O'Connell St), blown up by nationalists in 1966.

KILMAINHAM JAIL Inchicore Rd, Kilmainham, tel: 535984.
❏ 1100-1800 June-Sep.; 1400-1800 Wed., Sat. (Oct.-May). Bus 21A, 78A/B, 68, 69 from Fleet St; 79 from Aston Quay. ❏ £1.50, child 60p.
Former British jail where leaders of the 1916 Easter Rising (see **A-Z***) were executed. Political prisoners jailed here 1796-1924 included Parnell (see* **A-Z***) and de Valera (see* **A-Z***). Exhibits include cells and execution yard.*

GUINNESS VISITOR CENTRE Hop Store, Crane St, tel: 536700.
❏ 1000-1600 Mon.-Fri. Bus 21A, 78A/B from Fleet St. ❏ £1, child 50p.
Brewing museum with cooperage displays. Video show and a free glass of Dublin's finest (see **Guinness***) in a beautifully restored sampling area.*

IRISH JEWISH MUSEUM 3/4 Walworth Rd, tel: 534754.
❏ 1100-1500 Mon., Wed., Sun. (June-Sep.); 1030-1430 Sun. (Oct.-May). Bus 15A/B/C, 55 from College St to Harrington Rd. ❏ Free.
Documents, photographs and other memorabilia of Ireland's long-standing and influential Jewish community which includes Dublin-born Israeli President Chaim Herzog. Housed in a restored former synagogue.

PEARSE MUSEUM St. Enda's Park, Rathfarnham, tel: 934208.
❏ 1000-1230, 1400-1800 Feb.-Nov.; 1000-1230, 1400-1530 Dec., Jan. Bus 16 from O'Connell St (outside Clery's). ❏ Free.
Photographs, letters, memorabilia and audio-visual display tell the story of 1916 Easter Rising (see **A-Z***), led by national hero Padraic Pearse (see* **A-Z***) and others. Grounds are a 50-acre park with lake and nature trail.*

ABBEY TAVERN Abbey St, Howth, tel: 390307.
Bus 29A, 31 from Lower Abbey St. DART Howth. ❏ £3 (show only).
Stone floors and turf fires set the scene for a cabaret of Irish music and dancing, with dining. Swarming with Americans in summer. See **WALK 2**.

CLONTARF CASTLE Castle Avenue, Clontarf, tel: 332321.
Bus 30, 44A from Lower Abbey St. ❏ £7 (show only).
Decor of mahogany staircase and panellings in a Victorian castle setting. Casual, busy with locals and good value, with four acts nightly.

JURY'S IRISH CABARET Jury's Hotel, Pembroke Rd, Ballsbridge, tel: 605000. ❏ Tue.-Sun., May-Oct. Bus 46, 63, 84 from College St. DART Lansdowne Rd. ❏ £15.50 (show only).
Longest-running dinner/cabaret in town offers top-line Irish acts: comedians, crooners and balladeers, as well as traditional music and dancing.

DOYLE'S IRISH CABARET Burlington Hotel, Upper Leeson St, tel: 605222. ❏ Tue.-Sun., May-Oct. Bus 46 from College St, 46A/B from Fleet St. ❏ £15 (show only; inc. 2 drinks).
Also geared to the 'blarney and shamrock' view of Ireland beloved of American tourists but still an entertaining amalgam of modern and traditional music acts, plus comedy. Optional dinner features Irish dishes.

COMHALTAS CEOLTOIRI ÉIREANN 31 Belgrave Sq., Monkstown, tel: 800295. DART Monkstown/Seapoint. ❏ £1.50-4.
Traditional music, from the drone of the pipes to the roll of the bodhrán (hand-held drum), in a cabaret setting. With folk customs and dancing.

PINK ELEPHANT Setanter House, South Frederick St, tel: 775876.
❏ Full bar 2330-0230. DART Tara St, Pearse Station. ❏ £5.
Less 'in' than it might have been but still one of the best discos in town.

ANNABEL'S Burlington Hotel, Upper Leeson St, tel: 605222.
❏ 2200-0230 Tue.-Fri., 2030-0230 Sat. Bus 46A/B from Fleet St. ❏ £4.
Long-standing up-market disco in hotel plays mainstream music. Comfortable and not exclusively young. Unusually, has a full drinks licence.

Killiney Bay

Dublin Bay

Dublin Road

NORTH BULL ISLAND

ST. ANNE'S PARK

Howth Road

Malahide Road

N1 Swords Road

Ballymun Road

NATIONAL BOTANIC GARDENS

North Road

N2

Tolka River

Royal Canal

Navan Road

N3

River Liffey

PHOENIX PARK

R 109

Lucan Road

Grand Canal

Naas Road

N7

N4

N7

GARDEN OF REMEMBRANCE

ST. STEPHEN'S GREEN

N81

Merrion Road

Stillorgan Road

Rock Road

R 119

R 827

Bray Road

R 113

Sandyford Road

MARLAY PARK

Rathfarnham Road

Tallaght Road

N81

River Dodder

PHOENIX PARK

Bus 23 from Parnell Sq. East; 25, 26 from Middle Abbey St; 51 from
Fleet St, all to Parkgate St entrance.
*Largest park in Europe. Impressive, tree-lined central avenue runs past
lakes, deer herds, sports grounds. Always something happening. See* **A-Z**.

ST. STEPHEN'S GREEN

❏ 0800-dusk. DART Tara St, Pearse Station.
A great place to rest from the pace of the city centre. See **WALK 1**, **A-Z**.

GARDEN OF REMEMBRANCE Parnell Sq.

❏ 0930-2000 summer, 1100-1600 winter. DART Connolly Station.
*Quiet and peaceful garden opened in 1966 as a tribute to all those who
died for the cause of Irish independence. See* **WALK 1**.

NATIONAL BOTANIC GARDENS Botanic Rd, tel: 374388.

❏ 0900-1800 Mon.-Sat., 1100-1800 Sun. (summer); 1000-1630 Mon.-
Sat., 1100-1630 Sun. (winter). Bus 34/A from Middle Abbey St.
*Wide, varied collection of trees, shrubs, tropical plants and hothouses.
Walks on banks of River Tolka. Next to Prospect Cemetery (see* **A-Z**).

MARLAY PARK Grange Rd, Rathfarnam.

❏ 1000-1700. Bus 47B, 48A from Hawkins St.
*Extensive park of former country home, now restored. Nature trail,
woodlands set in suburban Dublin. Model steam railway. See* **CRAFTS**.

NORTH BULL ISLAND James Larkin Rd, Dollymount.

Bus 30 from Lower Abbey St. DART Killester.
*Miles of popular beaches, two golf clubs, bird sanctuary and information
centre. See* **Beaches**, **Birdwatching**, **A-Z**.

ST. ANNE'S PARK Mount Prospect Ave, Clontarf.

Bus 29A, 31/A/B from Lower Abbey St to Killester. DART Killester.
*Playing fields, gardens and woods, all set in grounds of mansion (now
demolished) of Lord Iveagh, of the Guinness family. Popular for walks.
Rose garden is a spectacular sight, best seen in June and early July.*

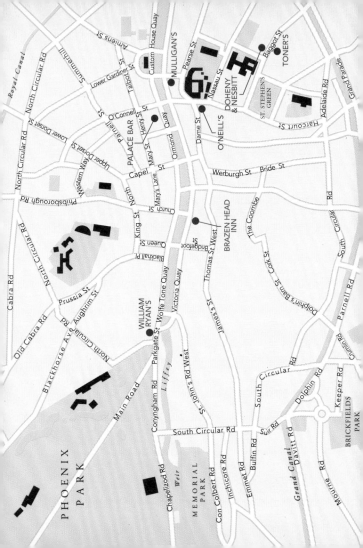

BRAZEN HEAD INN 20 Lower Bridge St.
❏ See **Opening Times**. Bus 21A, 78/A/B from Fleet St.
Oldest pub in Dublin, first licensed 1666 but said to date back to 13thC.
*Robert Emmett (see **A-Z**) is said to have planned his 1803 rebellion here.*

O'NEILL'S 2 Suffolk St.
❏ See **Opening Times**. DART Tara St.
High-gabled Victorian pub with an impressive clock outside. Bustling
and busy all day with bankers, students, the world and his or her dog.

MULLIGAN'S 8 Poolbeg St.
❏ See **Opening Times**. DART Tara St.
Dating back to 1845, this pub is dark, dowdy, bare – and a Dublin must.
Patronized by students and Irish Press staff. Contrary to the boast on out-
*side panel, it is not mentioned in Ulysses, but in Dubliners (see **Joyce**).*

WILLIAM RYAN'S 28 Parkgate St.
❏ See **Opening Times**. Bus 25, 26, 66/A, 67/A from Middle Abbey St.
Beautifully fitted-out bar, with four snugs, dark wood and old-fashioned
*lamps. Near Phoenix Park (see **A-Z**). Unchanged since turn of century.*

PALACE BAR 21 Fleet St.
❏ See **Opening Times**. DART Tara St.
Atmospheric bar of polished wood, mirrors, tiled floor. Stools or standing
in the main bar, chairs and tables in back bar and lounge. Mixed clien-
tele of working-class Dubliners and professionals. Smoky in evenings.

DOHENY & NESBITT 5 Lower Baggot St.
❏ See **Opening Times**. DART Pearse Station.
One of Dublin's famous names. Old-fashioned, with snugs and wood
panelling. The haunt of journalists, politicians, lawyers and architects.

TONER'S 139 Lower Baggot St.
❏ See **Opening Times**. DART Pearse Station.
200-year-old dark-wood bar with snugs and stone floor. Shelves and
drawers behind bar are a reminder of when pub doubled as grocer's.

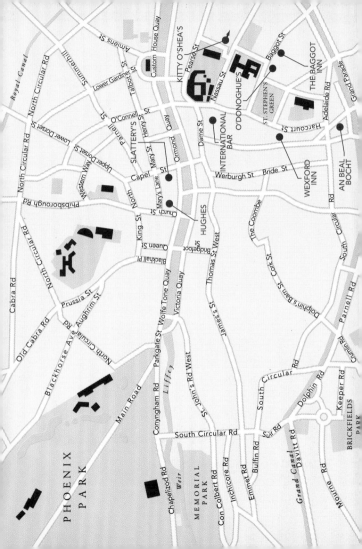

SLATTERY'S 129 Capel St, tel: 740416.
❏ See **Opening Times**. DART Tara St.
Dingy and full of character, with an interesting mix of folk and rock.

O'DONOGHUE'S 15 Merrion Row, tel: 607194.
❏ See **Opening Times**. DART Pearse Station.
*Famed for its impromptu traditional/folk sessions and great atmosphere.
Noted haunt of folk group The Dubliners. Ask first if you want to play.*

KITTY O'SHEA'S 23 Upper Grand Canal St, tel: 609965.
❏ See **Opening Times**. Bus 5, 7A from Eden Quay to Northumberland
Rd. DART Pearse Station.
*Trendy, busy pub with fine stained glass. Framed portraits of regulars
adorn the walls. Offers a traditional/folk music fare.*

AN BEAL BOCHT 58 Charlemont St, tel: 755614.
❏ See **Opening Times**. Bus 62 from Hawkins St. DART Pearse Station.
*Totally Irish pub where you are likely to hear the language. Small
enough to seem like someone's back room. Traditional/folk for purists.*

INTERNATIONAL BAR Wicklow St, tel: 779250.
❏ See **Opening Times**. DART Tara St, Pearse Station.
Venue for all up-and-coming rock bands, from heavy metal to New Age.

WEXFORD INN Wexford St, tel: 751588.
❏ See **Opening Times**. DART Pearse Station.
Specializes in traditional music in the Wolfe Tones, Furey Brothers vein.

THE BAGGOT INN Lower Baggot St, tel: 761430.
❏ See **Opening Times**. DART Pearse Station.
Dublin's main pub-rock venue. The city's best new bands play upstairs.

HUGHES 19 Chancery St, tel: 726540.
❏ See **Opening Times**. DART Tara St.
*Friendly pub and a well-known venue for traditional and folk music
every night. Also has Irish dancing.*

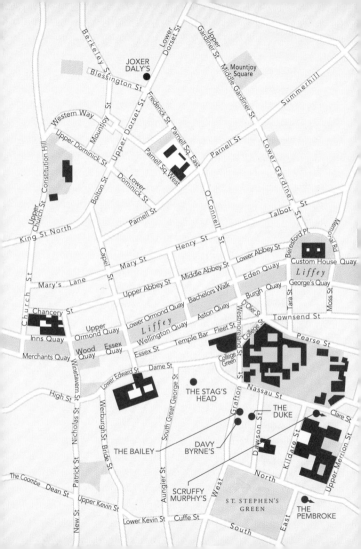

THE STAG'S HEAD 1 Dame Court, off Dame St, tel: 6793701.
❏ See **Opening Times**. DART Tara St.
Built in 1770 and remodelled (1895) into a classic Victorian bar and snug.
Mixed clientele includes Trinity students. Short menu is plain but tasty.

SCRUFFY MURPHY'S 1 Powerscourt, behind Mount St,
tel: 615006. ❏ See **Opening Times**. DART Pearse Station.
Trendy pub well-known among sportsmen and social high-flyers. Can be
tiresome when crowded. Refurbished, with a first-floor restaurant.

DAVY BYRNE'S 21 Duke St, tel: 711298.
❏ See **Opening Times**. DART Tara St, Pearse Station.
A landmark Dublin pub, where Leopold Bloom dined on Gorgonzola
*and Burgundy (see **Bloomsday**). The menu nowadays is more varied: try*
seafood sandwiches or Guinness and Galway Bay oysters.

THE DUKE 9 Duke St, tel: 774054.
❏ See **Opening Times**. DART Tara St, Pearse Station.
Gem of a pub now restored to its Victorian finery. Friendly and a great
place to drop in for a morning or afternoon coffee. Good-value snacks.

THE BAILEY 4 Duke St, tel: 6793734.
❏ See **Opening Times**. DART Tara St, Pearse Station.
A revered Dublin pub but after many facelifts it looks like a boring, mod-
ern bar. Varying menu, with the occasional oyster shucker on duty. On
*display is door of 7 Eccles St, home of Leopold Bloom (see **Bloomsday**).*

THE PEMBROKE 31 Lower Pembroke St, tel: 762980.
❏ See **Opening Times**. DART Pearse Station.
Does daily specials such as stew or chilli, as well as permanent menu,
which includes more unusual items like samosas. Sandwiches all day.

JOXER DALY'S 103 Upper Dorset St, tel: 305049.
❏ See **Opening Times**. DART Connolly Station.
Lovely pub noted for its lunches and snacks of typical pub fare. Superb
decor and a great place to have a couple of pints.

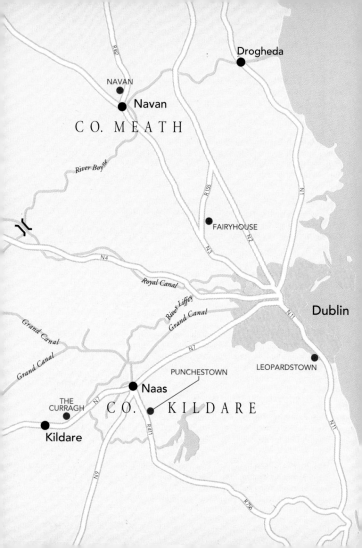

LEOPARDSTOWN Dublin, tel: 895686.
Take the N 11 (Stillorgan Rd) from city centre, through Kilmainham.
Bus 86 from Fleet St. 8 miles south of city centre.
A rarity these days, a racecourse in a city. The races at this ultra-modern course, originally built in 1888, are run against the picturesque back-drop of the Wicklow Mountains.

THE CURRAGH Co. Kildare, tel: 04-541205.
Take the N 7 (Naas Rd) from city centre. 30 miles west of Dublin.
The home of Irish racing, with the National Stud (see A-Z) and numerous training stables set on the vast Curragh plain. All Ireland's classic races are held here, including the Irish 2000 Guineas (May), 1000 Guineas (May), Derby (June), Oaks (July) and St. Leger (Oct.). Plays host to the world's richest race, the Cartier Million, from 1991 (Oct.) onwards. On race days special trains and buses run from Heuston Station (see Railways) and the Busaras, Dublin (see Buses).

FAIRYHOUSE Co. Meath, tel: 04-256167.
Take the N 3 (Navan Rd) to Black Bull. 16 miles north of Dublin.
This National Hunt course in an attractive setting hosts the Irish Grand National on Easter Monday. On race days special buses run from the Busaras, Dublin (see Buses).

PUNCHESTOWN Co. Kildare, tel: 04-597704.
Take the N 7 (Naas Rd) from city centre, through Kilmainham.
23 miles southwest of Dublin.
This attractive course near Naas is famous for its three-day festival meeting in late April. Special buses run from the Busaras, Dublin (see Buses), at festival time.

NAVAN Co. Meath, tel: 04-621350.
Take the N 3 (Navan Rd) from city centre. 30 miles northwest of Dublin.
The Troytown Chase is the best-known race run at this National Hunt course in a rural setting.

BAD ASS CAFÉ 9/11 Crown Alley, tel: 712596.
❑ 1130-2300 Mon.-Sat., 1200-2300 Sun. DART Tara St. ❑ Inexpensive.
Large, bright, buzzing place popular with students and budget eaters.
Children welcome. Try their pizzas rather than their pasta. In Dublin's
trendy so-called 'Left Bank' area of boutiques and cheap restaurants.

BURDOCK'S Werburgh St.
❑ 1700-2245 Mon., Wed., Fri., 1730-2245 Thu., Sat. DART Tara St.
❑ Inexpensive.
This traditional fish-and-chip shop is a Dublin institution. Fare is the
usual cod, haddock, ray, etc. but is superlatively cooked. Queues form
before opening time. No seating.

CORNUCOPIA WHOLEFOODS 19 Wicklow St, tel: 777583.
❑ 0800-2100 Mon.-Fri., 0900-1800 Sat. DART Tara St. ❑ Inexpensive.
Wholefood breakfast, lunch and supper are available in this restaurant at
the back of a busy shop selling health foods, herbs and spices.

NONNA'S 11 Merrion Row, tel: 611565.
❑ 1200-2400. DART Pearse Station. ❑ Inexpensive-Moderate.
Small, bistro-style Italian where pizzas are a better bet than pasta. Try
the Fiorentina *pizza (egg-topped) and delicious home-made garlic bread.*

LITTLE LISBON 2 Fownes St, off College Green, tel: 711274.
❑ 1700-2300. DART Tara St. ❑ Inexpensive-Moderate.
Small, with spartan decor, but always popular – sit all night if you want.
Unusual Portuguese/Angolan menu; try cataplana, *a delicious fish/shell-*
fish stew served in copper pot. Phone for table after 1900. Good, cheap
wines (some from Zimbabwe), or you can bring your own (no corkage).

BEWLEY'S 12 Westmoreland St, tel: 776761.
❑ 0800-1900 Mon.-Sat., 1000-1800 Sun. DART Tara St.
❑ Inexpensive-Moderate.
Breakfasts, lunches, dinners and snacks are served in a Victorian tea-
room ambience, complete with 'pinnied' waitresses. Known for their
cream cakes, pastries, bread and the best coffee in Ireland. See **A-Z**.

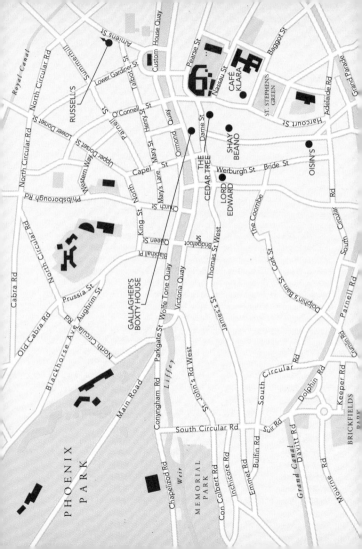

GALLAGHER'S BOXTY HOUSE 20/21 Temple Bar, tel: 772762.
❏ 0730-2300 (last orders). DART Tara St. ❏ Moderate.
Busy eatery with no booking – the maître d' will fetch you from The Auld Dubliner pub opposite when your table is ready. Great value, great food in pine-and-panelling setting. Try boxty (see **Food***) filled with beef, fish or chicken as a main course, or as 'dippities' (a starter with dips).*

THE CEDAR TREE 11 St. Andrew St, tel: 772121.
❏ 1730-2145 Mon.-Sat., 1730-2245 Sun. DART Tara St. ❏ Moderate.
Friendly, unhurried basement restaurant with Lebanese menu, similar to Greek fare. Home-made baklava (honey, nuts in pastry) is recommended.

LORD EDWARD 23 Christ Church Place, tel: 752557.
❏ 1230-1415 Tue.-Fri., 1800-2230 Tue.-Sat. DART Tara St. ❏ Moderate.
Well-appointed fish restaurant, full of character, with a great reputation.

RUSSELL'S Harbour Rd, Howth, tel: 322681.
❏ 1830-2230. Bus 31 from Lower Abbey St. DART Howth. ❏ Moderate.
Decor in this former harbour-side warehouse has a nautical theme and there is a discreet, cosy atmosphere, especially on cold, rainy nights. Fish, steak and chicken are offered à la carte or on a good-value set menu.

SHAY BEANO 37 Lower Stephen St, tel: 776384.
❏ 1900-2145. DART Tara St. ❏ Moderate-Expensive
Intimate, stylish and very French, this is one of Ireland's best restaurants. Creative nouvelle cuisine. Book for evenings, Fridays and Saturdays.

OISIN'S 31 Upper Camden St, tel: 753433.
❏ 1830-late Mon.-Sat. Bus 55, 83 from College St. DART Tara St, Pearse Station. ❏ Moderate-Expensive.
Leisurely, luxury dining can be had in this restaurant where Gaelic menus detail the traditional Irish fare. Seafood, steak specialities also available.

CAFÉ KLARA 35 Dawson St, tel: 778611.
❏ 1200-2315. DART Tara St, Pearse Station. ❏ Moderate-Expensive.
A large, stylish brasserie enjoying a good reputation. Fish is a speciality.

WHITE'S ON THE GREEN 119 St. Stephen's Green, tel: 751975.
❏ 1200-1430, 1900-2230 Mon.-Sat., 1900-2230 Sun. DART Pearse Station. ❏ Expensive.
Has a long-standing reputation as one of Dublin's finest for elegance, service and cuisine, ranging from traditionals such as Guinness and Oyster Pie to the more elaborate such as Chateaubriand in Truffle Sauce. À la carte or £25 set-price menu. Daily chef's special.

AYUMI-YA Newpark Centre, Newtownpark Avenue, Blackrock, tel: 831767. ❏ 1900-2300 Mon.-Sat., 1800-2200 Sun. ❏ Expensive.
Dublin's only authentic Japanese restaurant serves a varied menu.

LE COQ HARDI 35 Pembroke Rd, tel: 689070.
❏ 1230-1500 Mon.-Fri., 1900-2200 Mon.-Sat. Bus 5, 7/A from Eden Quay; 46, 63, 84 from College St. DART Pearse Station.
❏ Expensive.
Classic French cuisine and a fine wine cellar in the setting of a handsome Georgian house. This is big-spender territory.

THE GUINEA PIG 17 Railway Rd, Dalkey, tel: 859055.
❏ 1830-2230 Mon.-Sat., 1200-1500 Sun. DART Dalkey. ❏ Expensive.
Gourmet eating (as well as set menus and bar food): fish, game and Irish beef. Try Bradan Deilginnis (salmon stuffed with crab in lobster sauce).

KING SITRIC Harbour Rd, Howth, tel: 325235.
❏ 1830-2200 Mon.-Sat. Bus 31 from Lower Abbey St. DART Howth.
❏ Expensive.
Seafood restaurant set in a former terraced house in Howth. Game in season is a speciality but the restaurant is best known for its superb seafood, all bought direct from the local fishing fleet.

RESTAURANT NA MARA 1 Harbour Rd, Dun Laoghaire, tel: 806767. ❏ 1300-1415, 1900-2215. Bus 8 from Eden Quay. DART Sandycove. ❏ Expensive.
Gourmet seafood specialities in a converted Victorian railway station by Dun Laoghaire harbour. Attentive service and a touch of style.

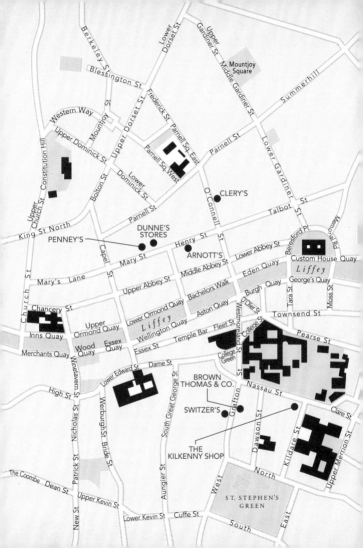

BROWN THOMAS & CO. 15 Grafton St, tel: 776861.
❑ See **Opening Times**. DART Tara St, Pearse Station.
*Exclusive store selling everything from saddles and clothing for the hunt
to the finest-quality household goods and men's and women's designer
fashions. Fine Victorian frontage.*

SWITZER'S 92 Grafton St, tel: 776821.
❑ See **Opening Times**. DART Tara St, Pearse Station.
*One of Dublin's famous shopping names. Their wide range of merchan-
dise includes clothing, leather goods, tableware and china, and the
entire Waterford Crystal product range (see* **Best Buys***).*

CLERY'S O'Connell St, tel: 786000.
❑ See **Opening Times**. DART Connolly Station.
*Impressive, turn-of-century brick building with superb brass nameplates.
Inside, a general department store with regular sales.*

DUNNE'S STORES Ilac Centre, Mary St, tel: 730211; also in St.
Stephen's Green Centre. ❑ See **Opening Times**. DART Connolly Station.
*Ireland's home-grown version of Marks & Spencer, selling similar ranges
of food, clothing and domestic goods. Renowned for its good value.*

THE KILKENNY SHOP 6 Nassau St, tel: 777066.
❑ See **Opening Times**. DART Tara St, Pearse Station.
*Small, quality store selling craftware like cut glass and hand-thrown pot-
tery, as well as a wide range of women's designer clothes, Aran knits,
cashmere and menswear (see* **Best Buys***). Their good upstairs café, overlooking Trinity College cricket ground, serves breakfast and lunch.*

ARNOTT'S 12 Henry St, tel: 721111; also in Grafton St.
❑ See **Opening Times**. DART Tara St, Connolly Station.
General store with restaurant. Strong on cosmetics and household linens.

PENNEY'S 47 Mary St, tel: 727788; other branches around the city.
❑ See **Opening Times**. DART Tara St, Connolly Station.
Cheaper chain store selling a wide range of clothing, household goods.

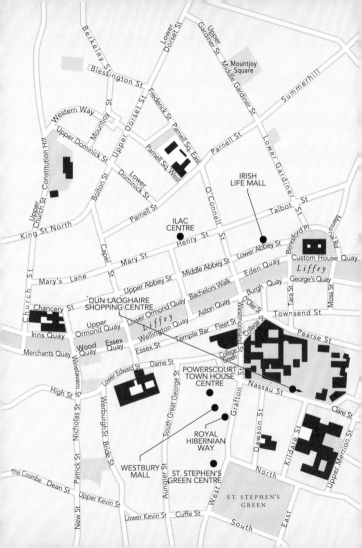

POWERSCOURT TOWN HOUSE CENTRE
Clarendon St, behind Grafton St. ❏ See **Opening Times**. DART Tara St.
200-year-old town-house complex combines a variety of restaurants,
including fish, vegetarian and French, with boutiques selling clothes,
jewellery, flowers and perfumes, all accompanied by live piano music.

WESTBURY MALL Clarendon St.
❏ See **Opening Times**. DART Tara St.
Part of the Westbury Hotel complex, this centre features diverse shops
selling antiques, fashion leather clothing, jewellery and Turkish carpets.

ROYAL HIBERNIAN WAY Between Dawson St and Duke Lane.
❏ See **Opening Times**. DART Tara St, Pearse Station.
Up-market, open-air arcade featuring designer clothing and shoes, hand-
made jewellery, hand-knitted sweaters, a bistro, a flower shop, etc.

ST. STEPHEN'S GREEN CENTRE King St South.
❏ See **Opening Times**; 1130-1700 Sun. DART Tara St, Pearse Station.
Large, modern centre with a light and airy atrium. Mainly clothing bou-
tiques but includes sports shops, bookshops, department stores, and
Sheils Balcony Restaurant (moderate prices). Parking.

IRISH LIFE MALL Lower Abbey St.
❏ See **Opening Times**. DART Tara St, Connolly Station.
Ground-floor mall featuring electrical-goods shops, Eason's stationers,
two reasonable cafés and a small, corporation-owned art gallery.

ILAC CENTRE Henry St.
❏ See **Opening Times**. DART Connolly Station.
Typical, bustling, down-market big-city mall with a combination of
cheaper department-store names and boutiques.

DUN LAOGHAIRE SHOPPING CENTRE Royal Marine Rd.
❏ See **Opening Times**; open to 2100 Thu., Fri. DART Dun Laoghaire.
Modern centre with 85 shops ranging from boutiques to chain stores.
Restaurants, pub with superb harbour views. Security parking. Crèche.

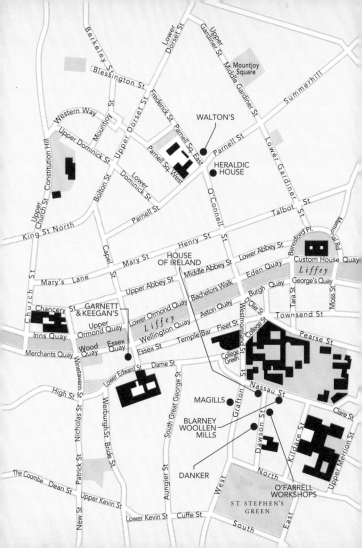

WALTON'S 2 North Frederick St, tel: 747805, freephone 1-800-600700. ❑ See **Opening Times**. DART Connolly Station.
Carries a range of new and second-hand electric and acoustic musical instruments, including Irish folk instruments. Music, records, cassettes.

GARNETT & KEEGAN'S 31 Parliament St, tel: 777472.
❑ See **Opening Times**. DART Tara St.
Clothes and sports goods for the country gentleman and lady.

BLARNEY WOOLLEN MILLS 21 Nassau St, tel: 710068.
❑ See **Opening Times**. DART Pearse Station.
*Top-quality woollen goods, including women's sweaters, coats, skirts, and hand-knits (see **Best Buys**). Men's and children's departments; gifts.*

MAGILLS 14 Clarendon St, tel: 713830.
❑ See **Opening Times**. DART Tara St.
Old-fashioned deli which stocks cured meats, pâtés, spices, sauces and teas. Enjoy the great smells and good browsing.

HERALDIC HOUSE 36 Upper O'Connell St, tel: 741133.
❑ See **Opening Times**. DART Connolly Station.
*Touristy selection of old Irish family trees and crests, as well as books and general guidance on tracing your family in Ireland (see **Genealogy**).*

DANKER 10 Anne St South, tel: 774009.
❑ See **Opening Times**. DART Tara St, Pearse Station.
Antique silver specialists, with a range of 19th and pre-19thC Irish silver.

HOUSE OF IRELAND Nassau St/Dawson St, tel: 716133/714660.
❑ See **Opening Times**. DART Tara St, Pearse Station.
A wide range of good-quality Irish craft and gift products.

O'FARRELL WORKSHOPS 62 Dawson St, tel: 770862.
❑ See **Opening Times**. DART Tara St, Pearse Station.
The ideal place to buy all your holiday mementos such as silver earrings, keyrings, T-shirts, bumper stickers, postcards and Irish honey.

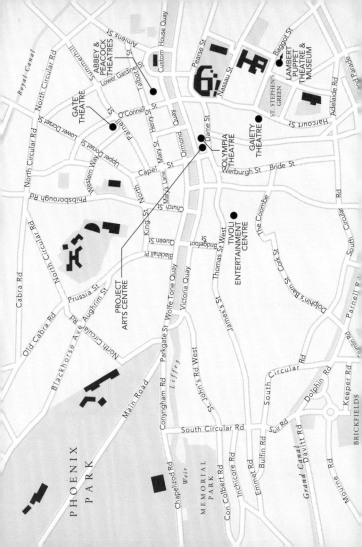

ABBEY & PEACOCK THEATRES Lower Abbey St, tel: 787222.
At terminus for north-side buses. DART Tara St, Connolly Station.
*Founded by Yeats (see A-Z) and others, the Abbey is Ireland's leading
theatre and very 'establishment', although the smaller Peacock (in the
basement) stages experimental, first-run and Irish-language plays.*

GATE THEATRE 1 Cavendish Row (Parnell Sq.), tel: 744045; credit
cards, tel: 746042. DART Connolly Station.
*Founded 1929 by writer/director Micheal MacLiammoir; Orson Welles,
James Mason were past performers. Known for avant-garde productions.*

GAIETY THEATRE King St South, tel: 771717.
DART Tara St.
*Ornate 1871 interior is backdrop for pantos, variety, TV shows, amateur
opera. Henry Irving, Beerbohm Tree and Ellen Terry all appeared here.*

OLYMPIA THEATRE Dame St, tel: 778147; credit cards,
tel: 778962. DART Tara St.
*Stately Victorian former music hall with superb interior where Laurel and
Hardy, Tyrone Power, John Gielgud performed. Presents drama, musicals.*

PROJECT ARTS CENTRE 39 East Essex St, tel: 712321.
DART Tara St.
*Leading fringe theatre noted for interesting experimental productions.
Also stages late-night stand-up comedy. See ART GALLERIES.*

TIVOLI ENTERTAINMENT CENTRE Francis St, tel: 544473.
Bus 21A, 78A/B from Fleet St. DART Tara St.
*Luxurious theatre which can be adapted for theatre-in-the-round. Leased
to professional companies, it presents a wide variety of productions.*

LAMBERT PUPPET THEATRE & MUSEUM Clifton Lane,
Monkstown, tel: 800974. Bus 7/A, 8 from Eden Quay. DART Salthill.
*Eugene Lambert, Ireland's best-known puppeteer and a regular performer
on TV, runs theatre and museum in the grounds of his own home. Shows
appeal especially to children. Telephone ahead to check schedules.*

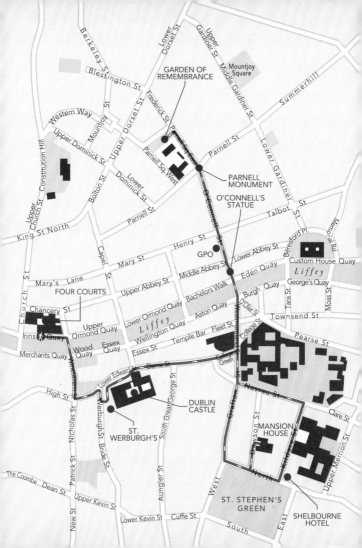

A two-hour walk around city-centre sites of importance in the struggle for Irish independence.

Start at Inns Quay, on the north
bank of the River Liffey, 1320
yards from O'Connell Bridge (see
A-Z). The green-domed building
dominating the quay is the Four
Courts, completed in grand style
by James Gandon in 1802 (see
BUILDINGS 1). The courts were
seized by the IRA in June 1922
during the Civil War (see **Ireland**)
and were badly damaged in a
subsequent Free State artillery
bombardment. They were restored

and reopened in 1931 and are still Ireland's main courts. Cross the
Liffey by the bridge on the left and walk up Winetavern St past Christ
Church Cathedral. Turn left into Christ Church Place and then right into
Werburgh St. 110 yards down on the left is St. Werburgh's, originally
founded in the 12thC and rebuilt in 1759. Its spire was removed in
1810 because it had been used as a vantage point for spying on Dublin
Castle (see **BUILDINGS 1**, **A-Z**) during Robert Emmett's (see **A-Z**) rising.
Emmett was hanged outside St. Catherine's in Thomas St, about 1100
yards to the west.

Retrace your steps up Werburgh St until you reach Castle St. Follow this
round to the second gate of Dublin Castle, the centre of British colonial
rule for centuries after it was first built as a fortress by King John in
1204. The castle has always been a focus for political intrigue: Red
Hugh O'Donnell escaped from the Birmingham Tower on Christmas
Eve 1591 (he was one of the leaders of the last great Catholic rebellion
against Elizabeth I, which ended in defeat in 1601 with the 'Flight of
Earls' to the Continent). In 1916 (see **Easter Rising**) the castle came
under fire from the rebels, who occupied various nearby buildings,
including the City Hall next door (see **BUILDINGS 1**). British soldiers
eventually managed to drive the rebels from their City Hall stronghold.

Follow Dame St towards the city centre and turn right into Grafton St, the city's main shopping area. At the top of the street is the magnificent St. Stephen's Green (see **PARKS & GARDENS**, **A-Z**) where nationalist forces under Countess Constance Markievicz, the first woman to be elected to the British House of Commons, were stationed during the 1916 Rising. Turn left and walk along the edge of the park until you reach Dawson St, at the top of which is the graceful Mansion House (see **BUILDINGS 2**), built in 1710 and now the Lord Mayor of Dublin's official residence. Here, the first free Irish parliament adopted the Declaration of Independence in 1919. Continue along the edge of St. Stephen's Green, and just beyond the junction with Kildare St is the imposing Shelbourne Hotel, where the constitution of the Free State was drafted in Room 112 in 1922. At the corner of the park opposite is a statue of patriot Wolfe Tone (see **A-Z**).

Turn back onto Kildare St and walk down to its foot. Bear left, following Nassau St into Grafton St and then straight on, up Westmoreland St and onto O'Connell Bridge. Ahead of you, in the middle of O'Connell St (see **A-Z**), is the 1854 statue of patriot Daniel O'Connell (see **A-Z**), who won Catholic Emancipation in 1829. Look closely at the winged Victories around the statue for bullet holes, souvenirs of the 1916 Rising.

Further up on the left-hand side of the road is the General Post Office, universally known as the GPO (see **A-Z**) and an everlasting symbol of

Ireland's struggle for independence from Britain. James Connolly (see **A-Z**) and Padraic Pearse (see **A-Z**) led the charge into the GPO on Easter Sunday 1916 to launch the week-long Rising. Pearse read the Proclamation of the Republic from the main door of what was by then the rebellion's headquarters. Fighting around the GPO was intense – you can still see where bullet holes were later filled in – and the building was reduced to a virtual shell by British artillery. Pearse and the badly wounded Connolly were taken from here to Kilmainham Jail (see **MUSEUMS**) and eventual execution with the 13 other leaders. Continue along O'Connell St. Many of the buildings damaged in 1916 were rebuilt in a variety of styles. Crass commercialism in the 1960s and '70s gave the street the reputation of a neon jungle but it is now beginning to recapture some of its 19thC grandeur.

At Parnell Sq., at the top of O'Connell St, is a monument to 19thC nationalist Charles Stewart Parnell (see **A-Z**) who fell from influence in a scandal as he was within sight of achieving Irish Home Rule from Britain. Cross the road into Frederick St and keep walking until you come to the Garden of Remembrance (see **PARKS & GARDENS**), a quiet haven in a busy capital city. The park was opened in 1966 to commemorate all who died for Irish freedom. The central sculpture by Oisin Kelly represents the mythical Children of Lir being transformed into swans. The walk ends here.

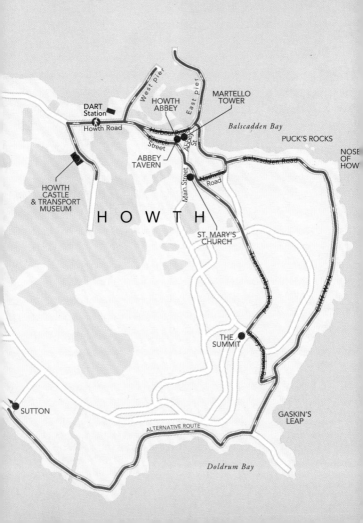

West pier

East pier

DART Station

Howth Road

HOWTH ABBEY

MARTELLO TOWER

Balscadden Bay

PUCK'S ROCKS

Harbour Road
Church Street

Abbey St.

ABBEY TAVERN

Balscadden Road

NOSE OF HOW

Nashville Road

HOWTH CASTLE & TRANSPORT MUSEUM

H O W T H

Main Street

ST. MARY'S CHURCH

Thormanby Road

THE SUMMIT

Carrickbrack Road

Ceanchor Road

SUTTON

GASKIN'S LEAP

ALTERNATIVE ROUTE

Doldrum Bay

A two-hour walk around the picturesque fishing village of Howth.

Start at Howth DART station. Turn right and walk back towards Dublin along Howth Rd for 250 yards until you come to the entrance to Howth Castle, a 14thC building remodelled by architect Sir Edwin Lutyens and now a hotel with its own golf course, on the opposite side of the road. Walk up the driveway past the famous garden of wild rhododendrons. The Transport Museum here has the last tram to run on the Sutton to Howth line, as well as antique lorries, passenger vehicles, an 1899 fire engine and a 1927 lorry used in the Oscar-winning film *Ryan's Daughter* (1400-1800 Sat., Sun., bank hol. 75p, child 25p. Tel: 475623).

Leave the castle grounds and walk back along towards Howth village. Ahead is the harbour with its walls pointing out towards Ireland's Eye, a small, uninhabited island just offshore. Just past the DART station, turn left down the west pier, alongside which Howth's fleet of fishing boats berths. They make an impressive sight tied up at weekends, often with the crews making essential repairs to the boats or their nets. By the pier are wholesale fish shops selling everything freshly caught, from salmon and oysters to mackerel and cod. They also sell to the public.

Return to Howth Rd. On the left is Howth Yacht Club, whose modern clubhouse sits incongruously alongside the large Victorian warehouses, now home to pubs and restaurants, on the other side of the road. Take Church St up the hill to the right, climbing steadily into the village, bearing to the left past the Garda (police) station. Opposite the Lighthouse pub is a good view of the harbour, Ireland's Eye and the Portmarnock Strand golf links: a good place for photographs. 200 yards further on are the preserved ruins of Howth Abbey, which dates from 1042. The roofless interior is locked but a key can be obtained from a nearby house – a sign gives details.

Carry on along Church St, past old houses and cottages and the Cock Tavern, a fisherman's pub, until you reach Main St. Go past St. Mary's Church, with its large rose window and the gargoyles on its tower. Take Thormanby Rd to the left. Here you have a choice of whether or not to tackle The Summit (Hill of Howth) where there is a 1stC Celtic cairn. If you would prefer not to, turn to p. 72 for the next part of the walk. If you choose the climb, continue up the steep, winding Thormanby Rd

to The Summit where the views, south towards Dublin Bay and the city or north over Howth Harbour, are splendid. At the top you can either catch a 31B bus back to the village or return via the spectacular but sometimes heart-stopping cliff walk. The walk is probably not advisable if you have young children or frail elderly people with you, and if you would prefer not to follow it, take the right-hand branch on the path when you join the cliff walk and continue around the head to Sutton, past the Bailey Lighthouse and Doldrum Bay, enjoying the spectacular view of Dublin Bay and North Bull Island (see **PARKS & GARDENS**, **A-Z**). At Sutton, take the DART or a 31, 31A or 31B bus back to Dublin.

To get to the cliff walk, take Bailey Garden Rd to the left and follow the path's left-hand branch to Howth at the remote Gaskin's Leap cliff. Follow the path round to the Nose of Howth promontory. 200 yards on, the path becomes Balscadden Rd just opposite Puck's Rocks. Join the shorter route (see below).

If you opt not to go on to The Summit, take Nashville Rd to the left and left on to Balscadden Rd, overlooking Balscadden Bay, with Puck's Rocks lying close to shore on the headland. Walk back down the hill, past the Martello tower (see **A-Z**) to the harbour and the east pier with

its lighthouse at the end. The 700-yard-long pier makes a bracing walk at any time but at dusk in the summer the view back towards the twinkling lights of Howth village and harbour are memorable. Follow Harbour Rd back round towards the main harbour. If you feel the need for refreshment, a quick detour up Abbey St to the left will bring you to the Abbey Tavern, a famous old pub with a flagstone floor, turf fires, and dating in parts from the 15thC (see **NIGHTLIFE**). Retrace your steps, turning left at the bottom of Abbey St to go back along Harbour Rd and finish at the DART station.

Accidents & Breakdowns: If you are involved in an accident where no-one has been hurt, exchange names, addresses and insurance details with the other driver. If there are any injuries, or you are in doubt about the validity of the information you have been given by the other driver, the Garda (police) should be called. In the event of a breakdown, AA members can call assistance from the AA breakdown services, tel: 770481. For other breakdown services, see the *Golden Pages* directory. See **Driving**, **Embassies**, **Emergency Numbers**.

Accommodation: Bord Fáilte, the Irish Tourist Board, grades its hotel and guesthouse accommodation. The top A* and A hotel grades include luxury castle hotels and city hotels, often with à la carte restaurants, while the bottom C grade hotels offer simple but acceptable accommodation. Most A grade guest-houses have *en suite* bathrooms and provide good-quality evening meals. Advance bookings (recommended for summer months and rugby-international weekends in January and February) can be made through Dublin & East Tourism, 14 Upper O'Connell St, tel: 747733. They have a range of publications detailing the types of accommodation and seasonal offers available. Rates are similar to, or slightly higher than comparable establishments in British cities, and prices are generally higher in summer. See **Camping & Caravanning**, **Youth Hostels**.

Airport: Dublin Airport is on the N 1 road north from the city. Aer Lingus, Ryanair and British Midland fly to a number of locations throughout Britain, while there are regular flights from other international airports throughout the day. For flight information, tel: 379900. The airport, which is in the middle of a multi-million-pound expansion programme, has modern facilities including a good restaurant, two bars and extensive duty-free shopping. A taxi ride to the city centre costs

£12-15, while the 41A bus runs between the airport and Eden Quay (90p, no banknotes). Aer Rianta, the airports authority, runs an express bus every 20 minutes during the day to the Busaras main bus station (see **Buses**) on Store St (£2.30, child £1.15).

Architecture: Dublin was the second city of the British Empire during the 18thC Protestant Ascendancy of the Anglo-Irish who possessed great wealth and influence which saw its expression in grand public buildings and houses. Architects like James Gandon, Francis Johnston and Edward Lovett Pearse worked with outstanding plaster workers like Michael Stapleton and James McCullagh. Many Georgian houses were pulled down between the 1960s and the mid-80s before planning laws were tightened but now fine terraces such as those on Merrion Sq., Baggot St and Marino Crescent, Fairview, are being restored.

A Georgian town house is distinguished by its four floors above a basement, with steps leading up to a large front door set in a handsome doorframe with a leaded fanlight above, a red-brick facade with rectangular, small-paned sash windows, and a slate roof. Outside are railings and other fine ironwork while inside, the beautifully proportioned rooms have stuccoed ceilings.

See **BUILDINGS 1 & 2**.

Baby-sitters: These are in short supply in Dublin. The *Golden Pages* lists a few child-minding and nanny services but your hotel reception desk is probably the best bet for finding a sitter.

Banks: See **Currency**, **Money**, **Opening Times**.

Beaches: Like other EC countries, Ireland is constantly battling with inshore water pollution, although the problem is almost totally confined to parts of the Dublin Bay area. Malahide and Portmarnock to the north and Killiney (see **EXCURSION 1**), south of Dun Laoghaire, are all superb beaches with good hygiene records. The beaches of North Bull Island (see **PARKS & GARDENS**, **A-Z**) are popular with locals but the grey-coloured sand can be off-putting. The broad sweep of strands around the bay also means that places like Howth (see **WALK 2**), Blackrock (see **EXCURSION 1**) and Killiney are ideal for long, bracing walks.

Beckett, Samuel (1906-89): Dramatist and novelist born in Foxrock, Co. Dublin, and best known for the play *Waiting for Godot*. His novels include *Molloy*, *Malone Dies* and *The Unnamable*. He was awarded the Nobel Prize for Literature in 1969.

Beggars: One of Dublin's shames is the large number of beggars, many of them children, on the streets – they are professionals, hanging around outside banks and pubs, hoping for the odd coin. Most Dubliners ignore them, so don't be afraid to tell them sternly to go away.

Behan, Brendan (1923-64): A writer as well known for his drinking sprees in haunts like McDaid's in Harry St as for his plays like *The Quare Fellow* and *The Hostage*. He was born near Mountjoy Sq. and lived most of his life in Ballsbridge.

Best Buys: Ireland's craft products continue to be of a high quality and popular with visitors. Pottery, jewellery and knitwear are particularly good buys. The pottery is often delicate, more fragile even than bone china – Donegal China and Belleek Pottery are the best-known types. Ireland is still one of the world's great crystal glass manufactur-

ers, despite production problems at the leading glassworks, Waterford. Other high-quality names are Galway, Dublin and Cavan, while new factories open up every year. Men's and women's clothes in wool, linen and tweed remain good value, particularly hand-knits from the west coast Aran Islands, and Donegal tweeds. Jewellery is usually based on Celtic designs or the Claddagh ring, with the crowned heart motif, a traditional love offering. See **CRAFTS**, **MARKETS**, **SHOPPING**.

BEW

Bewley's Oriental Cafés:
A Dublin institution for a century and a half, these cafés are popular places to eat, drink coffee or just waste time. Bewley's coffee is the best in the city and is made with whipped milk. The Quaker Bewley family started selling tea and coffee before 1842 and over the years opened cafés in Westmoreland St, South Great George St, Grafton St and Dundrum Shopping Centre. The family was bought out by Campbell Catering after financial problems in 1986. Grafton St is renowned for the mahogany and mosaic patterns on the facades but one of the hidden joys of Westmoreland St is sitting in the rays of the morning sun filtering through the stained-glass windows by the Fleet St back entrance. See **RESTAURANTS 1**.

Bicycle & Motorcycle Hire: Bicycles can be hired from a number of outlets, which are listed in the *Golden Pages*. Their main business is hiring to university students, so it may be difficult to hire out of term, particularly during the summer vacation. City-centre traffic is heavy and drivers often aggressive, so only the experienced and confident should attempt to cycle there.

Dealers include McDonald's Cycles, Wexford St, tel: 752586; Renta Bike, Lower Gardiner St, tel: 725399. Cost £20-30 per week.

Birdwatching: An unusual activity for short-term visitors to a city but the three exceptional locations in urban Dublin make it worth pursuing. North Bull Island (see **PARKS & GARDENS**, **A-Z**) was the country's first bird sanctuary and it has an impressive number of waders, ducks and geese, especially at high tide in winter, and an information centre. At Booterstown, between the main N 11 road and the DART railway line, a few acres of marsh provide a bird sanctuary, while tiny Dalkey Island is another haven for seabirds (see **EXCURSION 1**, **Dalkey**).

Bloomsday: On 16 June 1904, the fictional Leopold Bloom set out from the Martello tower (see **A-Z**) at Sandycove, a village on the coast south of Dun Laoghaire, at the start of a day's meandering through Edwardian Dublin. Author James Joyce's 'stream of consciousness' account of Bloom's adventures was recorded in the epic novel *Ulysses*, published in Paris in 1922 and a vivid depiction of the city at the time – many of the locations are still extant and the pubs still in business. Joyce aficionados now celebrate Bloomsday on the Saturday nearest to 16 June with a variety of walks, events and readings, which begin at the tower in Sandycove, now home to the Joyce Museum (see **EXCURSION 1**), and continue throughout the city during the day. Events centre on Merrion Sq. in the evening. See **Events**, **Joyce**.

Book of Kells: The chief treasure of Trinity College Library (see **LIBRARIES**, **A-Z**) where it is kept on public display in the Long Room. A beautifully illuminated Latin text of the four Gospels with flamboyant draughtsmanship and vivid colouring, its precise origins are uncertain, although it dates from about AD 800 and was brought to Trinity in 1661. It was originally one volume but was restored and rebound into four in 1953. One illuminated page and one of text are usually on display.

Bray: This Co. Wicklow holiday resort is now largely a dormitory town for Dublin. The seafront hotels, long promenade and harbour are relatively run down but the place still has a veneer of Victorian and Edwardian gentility. The town is the southern terminus of the DART (see **A-Z**).

Budget:

Cooked breakfast (café)	£1.50-2.50
Two-course lunch (pub)	£3-6
(restaurant)	£4+
Dinner for two	see **Eating Out**
Coffee	55p
Pint of Guinness	£1.50-1.75
Pint of premium lager	£1.75-1.90
Bus/DART (inner-city journey)	65p
Hotel room (per night)	£40-100
Cinema ticket	£2-3.50

Buses: Dublin Bus (Bus Atha Cliath) has a comprehensive network in the city, while Bus Éireann runs long-distance routes to the rest of Ireland. City buses are mostly double-deckers, coloured green-and-white. Services run either north or south of the city and only a few routes cross the River Liffey. Buses leave from and terminate at the streets around the north- and south-bank quays. All buses are driver-operated and it is best to have the correct fare (in coins if possible), although you can usually get change. A typical fare from the city centre to Clontarf or Rathmines would be 65p. Pre-paid tickets can be bought from shops in the city, and there are various weekly- and monthly-saver deals, including adult one-day rover tickets (£3), bus/DART rover (£3.50) and other combinations – details are available from tourist information offices (see **A-Z**) or Dublin Bus, 59 Upper O'Connell St, tel: 734222. Dublin Bus publish an excellent bus and tourist-information map (75p).

Bus Éireann services go from the Busaras, Store St, tel: 366111. Rover tickets, offering unlimited travel, cost £55 (£27.50 child) for 8 days, or £80 (£40 child) for a 15-day ticket. See **Transport**.

Cameras & Photography: All makes of film and equipment are available, as are good-quality processing laboratories and fast-processing shops. The post office processing service delivers prints free to anywhere in Ireland. There are no general restrictions on photography but ask first in a library or museum where the use of flash may be forbidden.

Camping & Caravanning: Camping is popular in Ireland but the only licensed year-round site near Dublin is at Shankill, about five miles from Dun Laoghaire and two miles from Bray. The site is comfortable, with all amenities. Charges are from £3.50-4.50 plus 50p per person. Mobile and holiday homes can also be hired; tel: 820011.

Canals: Both the Grand Canal, running through the south-side suburbs, and the Royal Canal, on the north side, were built in the 18thC for carrying freight to and from other parts of Ireland. They are now mainly used for leisure activities such as boating and fishing, and the restored and beautified Grand Canal banks from Dolphin's Barn to Ringsend are a popular walking route. The Royal runs through commercial and residential areas and is more run down.

Car Hire: This is expensive, so bring your own car if you can. Budget, tel: 420793; Avis, tel: 776971; Europcar, tel: 681777; and Hertz, tel: 767476, all have offices at the airport and in the city. Leading local companies include Argus Automobiles, tel: 904444, and Dan Dooley, tel: 772723. You should be over 23 years old and have held a full driving licence for at least two years with no endorsements. Collision-damage waiver costs a bit more but gives you full comprehensive cover. Typical rates are as follows: small car, £200-230 per week, £100-140 for three days; medium saloon, £270-310 per week, £180-200 for three days. Ask about cheap weekend deals when you are hiring. See **Driving**.

Chemists: Rules on selling drugs over the counter are stricter in Ireland than in Britain or the USA so you will have to ask the assistant for aspirin and other analgesics. The *Golden Pages* lists chemists open late (2200) and on Sundays in different parts of the city. O'Connell's, 55 O'Connell St, tel: 730427, is open 0830-2200 daily. See **Health**.

Christ Church Cathedral

Christ Church Cathedral: See **CHURCHES**.

Civil War: See **Ireland**.

Climate: Dublin's climate is moist and mild, although recent summers have been exceptionally dry. It can be very humid, as southwesterly winds blowing across the warm Gulf Stream are the main climatic influence. Snow is rare, though it can usually be seen on the surrounding mountains. July and August average temperature is 15°C, maximum 27°C; January and February average temperature is 5°C, maximum 10°C. Pack a light coat, jumper and umbrella even in summer.

College Green: No longer a green but still the meeting place for Grafton, Westmoreland, Dame and College Sts. The busy hub of the city, it is dominated by the Palladian west front of Trinity College (see **A-Z**) and the classical lines of the Bank of Ireland (see **BUILDINGS 1**). A favourite rendezvous place, with pavement artists and a large taxi rank.

Collins, Michael (1890-1922): Guerrilla leader and Director of Intelligence for the IRA before independence who had formerly worked as a civil servant in London. A bold and brilliant leader and charismatic personality, he is still revered today. He was the driving force behind the foundation of the Irish Free State and was Minister of Finance and Commander-in-Chief of the army. His death in an IRA ambush in Bealnablath, Co. Cork, during the Civil War (see **Ireland**) led to reprisals and is still a source of argument among historians and politicians.

Complaints: Any complaint you have should first be made to the manager of the premises, then to the Consumer Affairs Dept, Shelbourne Rd, tel: 606011. The Garda (police) Taxi Office deals with taxi complaints and licensing, tel: 732222. Although there is a growing official awareness of overcharging of both locals and visitors, the principle of caveat emptor still applies for most purchases.

Connolly, James (1870-1916): Born in Edinburgh, James Connolly was the founder of the Irish Transport and General Workers' Union and a revolutionary socialist who signed the Proclamation of Independence to lead his Citizen's Army during the 1916 Easter Rising (see **A-Z**). Badly wounded during the Rising, he was tied to a chair to be executed at Kilmainham Jail (see **MUSEUMS**).

Co. Dublin: The most populous of the Republic's 26 counties surrounds the city of Dublin and Dun Laoghaire. Co. Wicklow is to the south, Co. Kildare the west and Co. Meath to the north.

Crack: Not an illegal form of cocaine but a much-used word meaning a good time, e.g. 'The crack was good …', or 'The crack was 90 …'.

Credit Cards: See **Money**.

Crime & Theft: Like every city, Dublin has a crime problem, although the city centre is fairly safe at night. The usual advice applies: put valuables in hotel deposit boxes, don't flash money around, carry handbags and cameras close to you, and avoid lonely places, open squares and parks after dark. Pickpockets and bag-snatchers are the main problem, although not to the extent that they are in cities like Paris or Rome. Drivers should take special precautions when parking: never leave anything (even small things like sunglasses) in sight in the car, use a heavy and visible steering-wheel lock (many residents use a heavy steel chain and padlock), and conceal your radio. If you are robbed, try to find witnesses and report the incident to the Garda (police). Get a copy of your statement for insurance claims. See **Embassies**, **Emergency Numbers**, **Insurance**, **Parking**, **Police**.

Currency: The unit of currency is the pound or punt, which has 100 pence. Notes in circulation are £100, £50, £20, £10 and £5, and coins £1, 50p, 20p, 10p, 5p, 2p and 1p. The 50p, 10p, 2p and 1p are the same shape and weight as in the UK. See **Money**.

Customs Allowances:

Duty Paid Into:	Cigarettes	or	Cigars	or	Tobacco	Spirits	Wine
E C	300		75		400 g	1.5 l	5 l
U K	300		75		400 g	1.5 l	5 l

Dáil Éireann: The lower house of the Oireachtas (Parliament) to which a Teachta Dáil, or TD (MP) is elected. The leader of the government is the Taoiseach (pronounced 'Tee-shach'). The Seanad (Senate) is the upper house. See **Leinster House**, **Politics**.

Dalkey: A quaint seaside town south of Dun Laoghaire. Two castles, a medieval church and interesting shops and restaurants all combine to make Dalkey a fascinating day out. There are boat trips in summer from the harbour to Dalkey Island (see **Birdwatching**) where there is a Martello tower (see **A-Z**) and the ruins of an old church. See **EXCURSION 1**.

DART: Dublin Area Rapid Transport (DART) railway runs 0700-2330 for 23 miles around Dublin Bay between Howth (see **WALK 2**) in the north and Bray (see **A-Z**) in the south. The service is clean, cheap and regular with trains every five minutes at rush hour and every 15 minutes at other times. DART is linked to Iarnród Éireann (Irish Rail) and Dublin Bus services. Monthly and weekly saver tickets are available, with price dependent on route: ten-journey tickets, for example, are good value (e.g. ten 65p trips for £5.80). For timetable and fare information, tel: 363331 (0900-1715 Mon.-Fri.). See **EXCURSION 1**, **Buses**, **Transport**, **Railways**.

Dentists: See Health.

de Valera, Eamon (1882-1975): American-born nationalist who presided over the founding of modern Ireland and dominated Irish politics this century. He was a teacher at Blackrock College who took part in the 1916 Easter Rising (see **A-Z**) and was first president of Dáil Éireann (1919-21; see **A-Z**); president of the Irish Republic (1921-22); republican who opposed the 1921 Anglo-Irish Treaty and who helped start the Civil War (see **Ireland**); founder of Fianna Fáil (1926; see **Politics**) and the *Irish Press* (1938; see **Newspapers**); government leader or Taoiseach (1932-48, 1951-54, 1957-59); main author of the 1937 constitution; and president of the Republic (1969-73). The last prisoner to be released from Kilmainham Jail in 1924, he opened it as a museum in 1966 (see **MUSEUMS**).

Disabled People: Like many cities, Dublin is only just getting to grips with catering for disabled people. Kerbs are beginning to be sloped and lifts and ramps put in buildings as alternatives to stairs and escalators but in general facilities are patchy and change is a slow process. The National Rehabilitation Board, 25 Clyde Rd, Dublin 4, tel: 684181, publishes a comprehensive guide to the city which is a must for disabled visitors.

Drinks: Stout and whiskey remain the staple alcoholic drinks. Guinness (£1.50-1.75 a pint), brewed at St. James's Gate on Dublin's south side, is the most popular stout and far more satisfying than its Park Royal British cousin. Murphy's (from Cork) and Beamish (from Dundalk) stouts are also sold but they do not travel particularly well. Lagers are increasingly popular, and a wide range of European, Australian and American brands are brewed under licence, alongside Irish Harp. At upwards of £1.75 for a pint, prices for lagers are high. Real ale is non-existent in Dublin and the main beer, Smithwick's

GUINNESS

(£1.55-1.80), is gassy and sweet. Locally brewed Bass (£1.70-1.80) will be more to southern English tastes, while McCardles (of Dundalk) brew a fine bottled beer. Power's is the most popular Irish whiskey; others are Jameson's, Paddy and Bushmills. Irish coffee (with whiskey) is a popular winter drink, as are hot toddies (whiskey and lemon with cloves). House wine in pubs can be patchy, as in Britain. Tap water is safe to drink and there is a wide range of sparkling and still Irish mineral waters on sale, the best known being Ballygowan and Tipperary. Good-quality coffees and teas are on sale everywhere and can be ordered in any pub. See **PUBS**, **Guinness**, **Pubs**, **Whiskey**.

Driving: Valid driving licences of most countries are acceptable in Ireland. Attach a nationality disc and obtain a green-card extension to your insurance if you take your own car. Road rules are virtually identical to Britain: drive on the left, overtake on the right, give way to the right on roundabouts, and wear seat belts in the front. Speed limits are 30 or 40 mph in built-up areas and 55 mph on most other roads, although in practice Garda (police) speed traps are rare. Rural roads have a hard shoulder and it is polite to pull over if you are being overtaken. Drink-drive rules are the same as in Britain, although you are more likely to be stopped and tested in the country. Look out for cyclists and Dublin's notorious jaywalkers when driving in the city. The Irish Visiting Motorists' Bureau, 3 South Frederick St, Dublin, tel: 6797233, will help with any insurance problems. See **Accidents & Breakdowns**, **Car Hire**, **Parking**, **Petrol**, **Transport**.

Drugs: Dublin has a drugs problem, and penalties for possession and dealing are severe. If you are arrested for a drugs-related offence, contact your embassy (see **A-Z**). See **Emergency Numbers**.

Dublin Castle: A splendid melange of architectural styles, from the original early-13thC building commissioned by King John, to George's Hall, built for the visit of George V and Queen Mary in 1911. The castle dominates the old centre of Dublin and was the scene of numerous sieges and attacks over the centuries. The State Apartments, the Throne Room and the Chapel Royal are all richly endowed with history and exhibits, each one a showpiece in itself. The castle, home to British viceroys until the building of the Viceregal Lodge in Phoenix Park (see **A-Z**), was handed over to the provisional Irish government on 16 January 1922 by the last Viceroy, Lord Fitzalan. See **BUILDINGS 1**.

Dun Laoghaire: A port and busy commercial centre to the south of Dublin. Car-ferry services sail from here to Holyhead (see **Ferries**). The National Maritime Museum is located here. Dun Laoghaire's impressive granite harbour walls are popular for Sunday afternoon walks. See **EXCURSION 1**.

Easter Rising: The start of the final campaign which led to Irish independence was a purely Dublin affair. On Easter Sunday, 24 April 1916, about 1800 armed nationalists led by Padraic Pearse (see **A-Z**) of the Irish Republican Brotherhood and James Connolly (see **A-Z**) of the Citizen's Army seized Dublin's principal buildings. Their HQ was the GPO (see **A-Z**) on O'Connell St (see **A-Z**), where the Proclamation of the Irish Republic was read in a call to arms largely ignored by the people. Six days of action saw the British

army suppress the uprising with the widespread destruction of property by artillery and the death of more than 200 civilians. The British later executed the 15 leaders by firing squad at Kilmainham Jail (see **MUSEUMS**), creating martyrs and swinging opinion towards the rebel cause and independence, and away from the idea of home rule. The leaders are buried at Arbour Hill Cemetery in the city.

Eating Out: Dublin has a thriving restaurant business with plenty of choice, from the ever-present McDonald's to some of the most exclusive dining in Europe. Virtually every pub does some sort of food, from sandwiches to full, three-course meals. As Dublin is a university city, there are also a fair number of eateries serving cheaper fare such as pizza or pasta. Lunch is served from about 1230-1430 and dinner from 1900. Restaurants do not usually sell spirits and some have only wine licences. Set menus are generally better value than à la carte. Price categories in the **RESTAURANTS** pages are based on a three-course meal without wine for one person, and are as follows: Inexpensive – up to £10; Moderate – £10-20; Expensive – £20+. See **RESTAURANTS**, **Food**.

Electricity: 220 volts AC (50 cycles), so you can use British equipment without adaptors. Sockets are 3-pin flat or 2-pin round.

Embassies:

UK – 31 Merrion Rd, tel: 695211
Australia – Fitzwilton House, Wilton Terrace, tel: 761517
Canada – 65 St. Stephen's Green, tel: 781988
New Zealand – New Zealand House, London, tel: 071-9308422
USA – 42 Elgin Rd, tel: 688777

Emergency Numbers: 999 for all emergency services. Individual telephone numbers for Garda (police) stations are listed in the green section of the telephone directory. Other emergency numbers: Rape Crisis Centre, tel: 614911; Samaritans, tel: 727700; Alcoholics Anonymous, tel: 538998; Narcotics Anonymous, tel: 300944.

Bloomsday

Emmett, Robert (1778-1803): Nationalist leader who plotted revolt after the Union with Britain, in the Brazen Head Inn which still has his desk in an upstairs room (see **PUBS 1**). The 1803 uprising, which included an attempt to capture Dublin Castle (see **A-Z**), failed and Emmett was hanged outside St. Catherine's Church. He was buried in the cemetery at the Royal Hospital, Kilmainham (see **BUILDINGS 1**).

Events:

Last week in February-first week in March – Dublin Film Festival
17 March – St. Patrick's Day Parade (see **St. Patrick**)
Second week in April – Dublin Grand Opera Society Spring Season
End of June – Dublin Street Carnival
Last two weeks in June – Dublin Literary Festival (incorporating Bloomsday; see **A-Z**)

Third week in July – Carroll's Irish Open
Golf Championship
Second week in August – Dublin Horse
Show (see **Royal Dublin Society**)
Beginning of September – All-Ireland
Hurling Finals (see **Gaelic Games**)
Middle of September – All-Ireland Football
Finals (see **Gaelic Games**)
Second and third weeks in October –
Dublin Theatre Festival
End of October – Dublin City Marathon

Ferries: All sailings are popular, so book well in advance, particularly if you are travelling at a holiday period. Fares and services are competitive (return fare for an average-sized car, driver and up to three adult passengers averages between £130-160 depending on the season). Crossing times are approximately 4 hours to Wales and 2 hours 15 minutes to Scotland. Ferry operators are as follows: B & I, tel: 6797977 (Dublin-Holyhead, Rosslare-Pembroke); Sealink, tel: 808844 (Dun Laoghaire-Holyhead, Larne-Stranraer, Rosslare-Fishguard). Both companies' offices are at 16 Westmoreland St. P&O, tel: (Northern Ireland) 08-057474400 (Larne-Cairnryan).

Fishing: Sea angling is popular off Dun Laoghaire (see **EXCURSION 1**, **A-Z**), Howth (see **WALK 2**) and Skerries. Dublin's two canals (see **A-Z**) and the River Liffey also offer fishing throughout the year. A licence is necessary for all freshwater fishing, although price and conditions vary year by year. You can expect to pay about £25 for salmon, £15 for trout and up to £10 for coarse fishing. More information is available from the Central Fisheries Board, Balnagowan House, Mobhi Rd, Glasnevin, Dublin 9, tel: 379206. Fishing shops can also be helpful – try Patrick

Cleere & Son, Bedford Row, off Fleet St, tel: 777406. Rory's Fishing Tackle, 17A Temple Bar, tel: 772351, sells licences.

Food: Irish dishes can be found on many menus: local favourites tend to be seafood such as salmon (cheaper than in Britain), trout, shellfish and sea trout, much of it caught by boats out of Howth. Boxty, a type of potato pancake, is tasty, while some pubs serve boiled ham and cabbage, an Irish staple for generations. Irish bacon is as popular as ever, while soda bread, a wholemeal bread leavened with sodium bicarbonate, can be bought everywhere. See **RESTAURANTS**, **Eating Out**.

Four Courts: See **BUILDINGS 1**, **WALK 1**.

Gaelic: This is the Irish language. Many signs in the city are in Gaelic and it is taught in every school but you will only occasionally hear it spoken as more than just the odd phrase. Its daily use is strongest in the south and west of the country. The Gaelic League promotes the language and its use.

Gaelic Games: Hurling and football are administered by the Gaelic Athletic Association (GAA), founded in 1885. Both games are played virtually year-round, with the All-Ireland Finals held in September at Croke Park stadium, HQ of the GAA. Gaelic football, played with a round ball and similar to Australian Rules football, is a mixture of soccer and rugby. Hurling, which can be dangerous, is like hockey but the ball is played mainly in the air or carried on the flat end of the stick. See **Sports**.

Garda: See **Police**.

Genealogy: The starting point for anyone wishing to trace their ancestors is the Genealogical Office, 2 Kildare St, tel: 614877/611626. It's popular, so get there before it opens (1000-1230, 1400-1630 Mon.-Fri.). The National Library, also on Kildare St (see **LIBRARIES**), is another major source for documents. Bord Fáilte, the Irish Tourist Board, publishes an information sheet (no. 8), *Tracing Your Ancestors*, which lists other centres housing records (see **Tourist Information**). Don't be surprised if you have some difficulty in finding records – many were destroyed in the shelling of the Four Courts during the Civil War (see **Ireland**). If you want to hire a specialist research company, contact the Association of Professional Genealogists, 22 Windsor Rd, tel: 966522. See **SHOPPING 3**.

Golf: A local passion, with more than 20 courses in Co. Dublin, not to mention numerous pitch-and-putt courses. Deer Park is the only public 18-hole course but most clubs allow non-members to play, at least during the week. Among the top courses are: Deer Park Hotel, Howth Rd, Howth, tel: 322624 (four courses: 18, 12 par-3, 9, pitch-and-putt) – green fees £5.50, £7 weekend; Clontarf Golf Club, Malahide Rd, tel: 331520 – £13; Grange Golf Club, Rathfarnham, tel: 932889 – £18 (non-members weekdays only). Caddies and carts are rare commodities, so make arrangements in advance to hire them. Bord Fáilte, the Irish Tourist Board, publishes a helpful information sheet (no. 38; see **Tourist Information**), or contact the Golfing Union of Ireland, 81 Eglinton Rd, tel: 694111.

GPO (General Post Office): Dominates O'Connell St (see **A-Z**) and is commonly known by its initials. It was built in 1818 in neo-Grecian style with an Ionic portico of fluted columns topped by John Smyth's figures of Hibernia, Mercury and Fidelity. It was the HQ for the 1916 Easter Rising (see **A-Z**), the Proclamation of the Republic being read from its steps, and it remains a reviewing point for marches and processions, as well as the city's main post office. Inside is a bronze statue centrepiece of Cuchulain, a legendary hero from Celtic myth. The marble plinth bears the words of the Proclamation and the names of its signatories (0800-2000 Mon.-Sat., 1030-1830 Sun.). See **WALK 1**.

Guinness: In 1759 Arthur Guinness brewed 200 hogsheads of ale and went on to found a dynasty whose name is synonymous with everything Irish, even though the company is now British-owned. The Guinness reputation is based on its famous dark stout, originally brewed as porter, then much favoured by the porters of London's Covent Garden. The St. James's Gate site near the Liberties district on the south bank of the Liffey covers 60 acres and is one of the biggest breweries in the world. The wealthy Guinness family have been major benefactors of the city over the years, contributing, among other things, to the restoration of St. Patrick's Cathedral (see **CHURCHES**). Although brewed in 16 other countries, it's said Guinness tastes best in Dublin – and contrary to rumour, it is not made from Liffey water. Drawing a pint is regarded as a skill – after ordering, you will have to wait at least five minutes before your drink is ready to be served. See **MUSEUMS**.

Halfpenny Bridge: The metal footbridge across the Liffey which is one of the strongest symbols of the city for locals and visitors alike. Built in 1816 and first called the Wellington Bridge, its proper name is the Liffey Bridge. Its common name (pronounced 'Ha'penny') comes from its former half-penny toll.

Health: Visitors from EC countries and their families on holiday or on short business trips to Ireland can get urgent medical treatment in the same way as an Irish national with a medical card – in practice this is the same as the NHS in Britain. Visitors from the UK will need to give their home address and their national-insurance number to the doctor or hospital, while those resident in other EC countries should present form E 111. Non-EC visitors will have to pay the full rate.
Six hospitals are on 24-hour emergency call: North side – James Connolly Memorial, Blanchardstown, tel: 213844; Mater, Eccles St, tel: 301122; Beaumont, Beaumont Rd, tel: 377755. South side – St. James's, Kilmainham, tel: 537941; Meath, Heytesbury St, tel: 536555; St. Vincent's, Elm Park, tel: 694533. There is an on-call emergency dentists' rota – details from any of the above hospitals' accident and emergency departments. See **Chemists, Disabled People, Emergency Numbers, Insurance**.

Horse Riding & Trekking: There are many stables in the city and surrounding areas offering both showjumping and trekking packages. Information is available from the Irish Horse Board, Irish Farm Centre, Naas Rd, tel: 501166, or the information sheet (no. 65) published by Bord Fáilte, the Irish Tourist Board (see **Tourist Information**). The following centres offer trekking: Castleknock Equestrian Centre, College Rd, Castleknock, tel: 201104, in Phoenix Park; Inchanappa House, Ashford, Co. Wicklow, tel: 0404-40230, in the Wicklow Mountains.

Horses: Many Dubliners, like other Irish people, have a fascination with horses. Horse-drawn carts carrying scrap metal are still a common sight in the city and on the first Sunday of each month there is a lively trade in horses and donkeys at Smithfield Market. Many of the ponies for sale at the market are bought by youngsters from housing estates to the north and west of the city, where the animals graze in gardens and on grass verges, and are ridden bareback by their owners. At the other end of the social spectrum, the Dublin Horse Show, held at the Royal Dublin Society (see **A-Z**) grounds in Ballsbridge every August, is a top-rank international showjumping event, attracting 1500 horses and their riders to compete in some 90 events. There are a number of racecourses in Co. Dublin, including Leopardstown in the city itself, although the famous Phoenix Park course has now closed. See **RACECOURSES**.

Howth: See NIGHTLIFE, RESTAURANTS 2 & 3, WALK 2.

Insurance: You should take out travel insurance covering you against theft and loss of property and money, as well as medical expenses, for the duration of your stay. A travel agent should be able to recommend a suitable policy. See **Crime & Theft**, **Driving**, **Health**.

Ireland: The island developed as an early Christian centre ('holy Ireland') in Celtic times but its history has been dominated for the past thousand years by battles with invaders: first the Vikings (see **A-Z**), then the Normans who established their rule based on Dublin (the Pale). In the countryside Irish chieftains continued to rule (beyond the Pale) in the four provinces: Ulster (north), Connacht (west), Munster (south) and Leinster (east). Finally, the English began colonization during Elizabeth I's reign, encouraging Presbyterian settlers to the north of the island and sowing the seeds of the religious troubles which still plague politics and society there. Ireland's history from then until the 20thC was dominated by a slow struggle for independence from British rule (see **WALK 1**), finally achieved after the 1921 Anglo-Irish Treaty but only at the cost of

Britain's retention of six of the 32 counties as Northern Ireland. The treaty led to the Civil War, which started in June 1922 and lasted for 11 months as the Irish Republican Army battled with the ultimately victorious army of the Irish Free State. Parts of Dublin, including the Four Courts (see **BUILDINGS 1**) and the Customs House (see **BUILDINGS 2**), were badly damaged in the fighting.

The Free State severed the last of its colonial ties with Britain to become the Republic of Ireland in 1949. Since joining the European Community in 1973, Ireland has tended to emphasize its European outlook, and it held the Presidency of the EC in 1990. See **Politics**.

Joyce, James (1882-1941): There is something perverse about how a man who derided the city of his birth to such an extent can now be so revered and used to promote its tourism industry. Such is the lot of James Joyce, whose most famous book, *Ulysses*, published in 1922, described a day in the life of Dublin. An experimental work which is often heavy going – neither Yeats nor Shaw could finish it – *Ulysses* has nevertheless had a lasting influence on the modern novel. It is Joyce's most famous work and a name which is impossible to avoid in the city, and indeed is the reason why many people visit. You can take a *Ulysses* tour following the book's route, join in the Bloomsday (see **A-Z**) celebrations, or simply visit Davy Byrne's, the 'moral' pub where Leopold Bloom, the book's main character, had a glass of Burgundy with some Gorgonzola sandwiches. His other work, particularly *Dubliners*, *Portrait of the Artist as a Young Man* and *Finnegans Wake*, helped establish Joyce as a major writer who is now widely celebrated in Dublin, not least on Bloomsday and at the Joyce Museum (see **EXCURSION 1**).

Laundries: Hotels usually have their own laundry service, while the *Golden Pages* also list laundries and launderettes. Most are closed on Sundays. The following have self-service machines and also do service washes: Blue Star Cleaners, 6 Terenure Rd, Rathgar, tel: 909344; The Laundry and Dry Cleaning Shop, 365 North Circular Rd, tel. 308558.

Leinster House: Built in 1745-48 by Richard Cassels as the lavish town house of Lord Kildare, who became Duke of Leinster in 1766. The house was sold in the early 19thC to the Royal Dublin Society (see **A-Z**), ultimately becoming the home to parliament in 1922. Entry to the Dáil (see **A-Z**) or Seanad (Senate) visitors' galleries is available only by ticket from a TD (MP) or Senator, obtained directly or through your embassy (see **A-Z**).

Licensing Laws: Normal pub hours are 1000-2300 (2330 in summer) Mon.-Sat., 1200-1400, 1600-2300 Sun., with 30 minutes' drinking-up time. Some pubs open at 0730 but shut earlier, while many discos and clubs serve alcohol in one form or another into the night.

Restaurants and discos often serve only wine. The famous 'holy hour', which forced people out of the pubs and back to their offices and workplaces, now exists only on Sunday and is two hours long, from 1400-1600. Licensing laws are standard across Ireland, although pubs can be found everywhere which open at more convenient illegal hours.

Literary Dublin: Small cities need to make much of their particular speciality, and Dublin's is writers. Swift (see **A-Z**), Sheridan, Burke, Moore, Wilde (see **A-Z**), Synge (see **A-Z**), Joyce (see **A-Z**) and O'Casey (see **A-Z**) have their reputations secured, while the more recent Behan (see **A-Z**), Kavanagh, O'Brien and Donleavy are widely respected. Two Dubliners, Yeats (see **A-Z**) and Shaw (see **A-Z**), won Nobel Literature Prizes in the 1920s as did another, Beckett (see **A-Z**), in 1969. The tradition continues with newer writers such as Dermot Bolger and Maeve Binchey. Dublin's creativity over the years is an immense field for study and no interested visitor will be disappointed by the sources of information, be they libraries, bookshops, newspapers, pub talk or a stranger on a bus. See **BOOKSHOPS, LIBRARIES**.

SENATOR
WILLIAM BUTLER YEATS
1865-1939
POET & PLAYWRIGHT
LIVED HERE
1922-1928

SENATOR
OLIVER ST. JOHN GOGARTY
(1878 – 1957)
SURGEON, POET, STATESMAN
WAS BORN
IN THIS HOUSE.

1779
THE BIRTHPLACE OF
THOMAS MOORE
IRELAND'S LYRIC
POET
RECONSTRUCTED IN 1963

DUBLIN AND EAST TOURISM
JOSEPH
SHERIDAN
LE FANU
1814 - 1873
WRITER
LIVED HERE

Lost Property: The best bet is a visit to the Garda (police) station nearest to where you think you lost the item, or contact the central lost property section for the city at Harcourt Sq. Garda station, tel: 732222. If you think you lost something on a bus or a DART train, contact Dublin Bus, 59 Upper O'Connell St, tel: 720000. See **Insurance**.

Martello Towers: When the fear of invasion by Napoleon was at its height in the early 1800s, a string of observation forts was built around the coasts of Britain and Ireland. These towers had a 360-degree field of vision and were heavily armed – but the invasion never came. Some have since become homes and museums, such as the Joyce Museum in Sandycove (see **EXCURSION 1**).

Money: Major credit and charge cards are universally accepted, while traveller's cheques in major currencies can be changed at any of the numerous bureaux de change in the city centre – compare rates first, however. Some places also accept British sterling notes and cheques supported by a banker's card but you will probably not get the full exchange rate. See **Crime & Theft**, **Currency**.

Music: Dublin is a thriving music centre, producing a string of top-line acts over the years, including The Dubliners, Boomtown Rats, U2, The Pogues and Sinead O'Connor. All types of live music are available, from classical, rock and jazz to country, Irish traditional and heavy metal. Venues range from pubs and hotels to the National Concert Hall, Earlsfort Terrace, tel: 711533, where the RTE Orchestra (see **Television & Radio**) regularly performs classical concerts. Traditional music is nurtured by Comhaltas Ceoltóiri Éireann, the Fellowship of Musicians of Ireland, which has regular sessions or ceilidhs at its Monkstown headquarters. Pubs like O'Donoghue's feature modern folk groups, while those like the Baggot Inn showcase the best of Ireland's rock bands. Impromptu jam sessions are more likely at folk venues – ask before you join in. Ireland is a regular stopping-off point for international rock tours, often at the Point Depot, North Wall Quay, tel: 363633. *Hot Press* and *In Dublin* (see **What's On**) have comprehensive listings, and most music shops sell tickets for shows. See **NIGHTLIFE**, **PUBS 2**.

National Museum of Ireland:
A wonderfully varied collection
which deserves a visit even if your
time is short. Displays range from
the Iron and Bronze Ages to ancient
Egyptian, Roman and Viking times.
There are examples of 17thC
Dublin silverware, 18thC clothing

and old musical instruments.
The Presidential Room displays items connected with
Ireland's presidents, while
another collection features
memorabilia dealing with
the 1916 Easter Rising (see **A-Z**) and its main characters. But it is the
Treasury where the real wealth of the museum is found. Its display (for
which a charge is payable) features some of the best pieces of early
Christian art anywhere, including the Ardagh Chalice (8thC) and the
Derrynaflan Chalice (9thC). See **MUSEUMS**.

National Stud: Based at Tully, Co. Kildare, near The Curragh (see
RACECOURSES) and dedicated to raising the standard of Irish bloodstock.
The stud includes research laboratories and a horse-racing museum, as
well as Japanese gardens, exquisitely laid out to symbolize the life of
man. There is a bonsai centre, café and shop on site. 1030-1700 Mon.-
Fri., 1030-1730 Sat., 1400-1730 Sun., Easter-Oct. £2, child £1 for both
stud and gardens.

Newspapers: There are four national daily newspapers and three Sundays. The *Irish Times* is politically independent, the most serious and usually has the best coverage of Dublin's cultural scene. The *Irish Independent* tends more towards Fine Gael (see **Politics**) and is owned by a group led by Heinz boss Tony O'Reilly. The tabloid *Irish Press* was founded by Taoiseach and later president Eamon de Valera (see **A–Z**) to give a Fianna Fáil view (see **Politics**) and is still part-owned by his family. Both the *Independent* and the *Press* have Sunday editions, while both groups also produce evening newspapers, the *Herald* and the *Evening Press* respectively. The politically independent *Sunday Tribune* makes up the list of national titles. The *Cork Examiner* and the *Belfast Telegraph* also publish daily. Some British newspapers (e.g. *Daily Mirror*, *Daily Star*, *Sunday Times*) publish Irish editions and virtually all are on sale the same day at newsagents across the city at set Irish punt prices – the best selection is at Eason's on O'Connell St. See **What's On**.

Nightlife: Dublin offers everything in the way of entertainment you would expect from a thriving European capital. There are many cinemas and live-music venues, as well as the theatre which is such a cherished part of the city's cultural heritage. Dinner shows with Irish

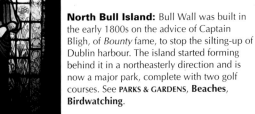

balladeers remain popular, and there are numerous discos and nightclubs but they constantly change venue and name as styles and fashions change. The main nightlife, as in the rest of Ireland, however, is in the pub, the centre for talk, music, drinking and general crack. See **NIGHTLIFE, PUBS, THEATRES, Music, Pubs**.

North Bull Island: Bull Wall was built in the early 1800s on the advice of Captain Bligh, of *Bounty* fame, to stop the silting-up of Dublin harbour. The island started forming behind it in a northeasterly direction and is now a major park, complete with two golf courses. See **PARKS & GARDENS, Beaches, Birdwatching**.

O'Casey, Sean (1880-1964): Brought up in Dublin's northside tenement slums and self-educated, he displayed great insight and wit as a writer of plays about the city's ordinary people and their troubles. He was almost 40 when his first play was accepted by the Abbey Theatre (see **THEATRES**) but he made his reputation with his second Abbey production, *Juno and the Paycock*, which is still performed regularly. *The Plough and the Stars*, based on the 1916 Easter Rising (see **A-Z**), caused riots at its first performance. O'Casey left Ireland in 1928 for the south of England, where he wrote a lengthy six-volume autobiography, from *I Knock at the Door* to *Sunset and Evening Star* before his death.

O'Connell, Daniel (1775-1847): Known as 'The Liberator', he was leader of the nationalist struggle for constitutional reform which led to Catholic Emancipation in 1829. He later became the first Catholic MP in the British House of Commons, then first Catholic Lord Mayor of Dublin. He is commemorated by an 1854 bronze figure by Irish sculptor John Henry Foley in O'Connell St (see **A-Z**) and a tall tower in Prospect Cemetery (see **A-Z**), where he is buried.

O'Connell St & Bridge: Both are named after Daniel O'Connell (see **A-Z**). In the mid-18thC, work began to widen an existing road going north from the Liffey and create a grand, residential boulevard more than 130 ft wide. Much of it was destroyed by British artillery during the 1916 Easter Rising (see **A-Z**) and the Civil War (see **Ireland**) but it was later rebuilt to near its former grandeur. Neon lights, garish shop fronts and the opening of numerous fast-food outlets gave the street a poor image and tawdry appearance during the 1970s, something which Dublin corporation is now trying to reverse. The central walkway of the street is tree-lined and has a series of statues and memorials, including those to trade-union leader Jim Larkin and Victorian nationalist leader Charles Stewart Parnell (see **A-Z**).
The bridge over the Liffey was built in 1880, replacing James Gandon's 1794 Carlisle Bridge, and it is unusual in being broader than it is long. It is Dublin's axis, linking the traditionally affluent south side and more artisan north side (although this distinction itself is fast disappearing). See **WALK 1**.

Opening Times:
Banks – 1000-1230 Mon.-Fri., 1330-1500 Mon.-Thu., 1330-1700 Fri.
Churches – Catholic churches are open all day; Church of Ireland
churches generally open only for services.
GPO – 0800-2000 Mon.-Sat., 1030-1830 Sun.
Post offices – 0900-1700 Mon.-Sat.
Pubs – 1000-2300 Mon.-Sat. (2330 in summer), 1200-1400, 1600-
2300 Sun., with 30 minutes' drinking-up time.
Shops – 0900-1730 Mon.-Sat., with some Thu. opening to 2200.

Orientation: The River Liffey and O'Connell Bridge (see **A-Z**) are the
hub of Dublin and the points from which the city orientates itself. South
side postcodes are even and north side odd, and almost all bus routes
keep to one or other side of the river (see **Buses**). Dublin's street layout
is not easy to follow, so it's best to buy a map: Dublin Bus publish a
good city-centre tourist-information and route map (75p), and the
pocket-sized Ordnance Survey map, while more expensive, is also
comprehensive.

Parking: Dublin has a desperate shortage of parking spaces, both on the streets and in car parks. There are time restrictions for on-street parking but explanation signs are almost non-existent, so look at the yellow lines: double lines mean no parking, single lines mean parking is permitted after 1800. Traffic wardens patrol the inner city area but there is still widespread parking on double-yellow lines and on the pavement, particularly after the wardens go off duty at 1800. Parking your car half on the pavement is acceptable in many places, particularly residential areas – look at what the locals are doing. In the city centre you should use an official car park with supervisors – you may have difficulty finding a place but it will be more secure than parking on unofficial sites or on wasteland, where your vehicle will almost certainly be broken into. Never leave anything on view in the car and use a heavy-duty anti-theft device. If a youngster offers to watch your car, say 'yes' and tip him £1 when you return. Your car will be untouched – it won't be if you refuse the offer. Official car parks around the city centre can be found at: St. Stephen's Green Centre, Ilac Centre, Marlborough St, Cathal Brugha St, Frederick Lane and Drury St. Car parks usually charge a flat rate of 50-65p per hour. See **Driving**.

Parliament: See **Dáil Éireann, Leinster House**.

Parnell, Charles Stewart (1846-91): Born in the beautiful mansion of Avondale, Co. Wicklow, where he lived most of his life and which is now a museum (see **EXCURSION 2**). He was an Anglo-Irishman who became MP for Meath at the age of 29 and fought at Westminster for the rights of small farmers. As president of the Land League he developed the policy of blacklisting and campaigning against absentee landlords who evicted Irish peasants from smallholdings. This 'boycotting' policy was named after one of its victims, a Captain Boycott. He became the leader of the Home Rule movement, winning support from prime minister William Gladstone despite a brief term of imprisonment in Kilmainham Jail (see **MUSEUMS**). He fell from power when his enemies used his long-term relationship with Katherine O'Shea (known to history as Kitty O'Shea), wife of another politician, to discredit him. He was forced out as party leader and died shortly afterwards. He is buried in Prospect Cemetery (see **A-Z**) and is commemorated in a memorial by Dublin-born Augustus Saint-Gaudens at the north end of O'Connell St, by Parnell Sq. (see **WALK 1**).

Passports & Customs: British citizens born in the UK and travelling from Britain do not need passports, although it is advisable to take one, or another form of photographic identification. Nationals from other countries must have a valid passport, while some (not EC countries, Australia, Canada, New Zealand or USA) also need visas – details from Irish consulates, embassies or tourist information offices. Travellers (including those going to Northern Ireland) must have been outside the Republic for at least 36 hours before they will be allowed to claim duty-free allowances on return to the country. See **Customs Allowances**.

Pearse, Padraic (1879-1916): A member of the paramilitary Irish Republican Brotherhood who on Easter Monday 1916 read the rebellious Proclamation calling on Irish citizens to fight for freedom from British rule. After the crushing of the Rising by the British he was taken to Kilmainham Jail (see **MUSEUMS**) where he was executed. Mementos of his life are displayed in the National Museum (see **MUSEUMS**, **A-Z**) and Pearse Museum (see **MUSEUMS**). See **Easter Rising**.

Petrol: Petrol is more expensive than in the UK, although unleaded is much cheaper than four-star. Maximum prices are set by the government each month and most garages charge the full price although there is some competitive price cutting. See **Driving**.

Phoenix Park: The pride of Dublin and, at 1750 acres, bigger than London's six major parks put together. In 1747, public access was granted to what had been a royal deer park and generations since have enjoyed Phoenix Park, which is popular for sports (polo, cricket, gaelic games, soccer and running), sightseeing and walks through unspoiled countryside. Enter by the main gate (Parkgate St) by the Liffey at the southeast corner. Places of interest are clearly marked: the People's Garden, a formal garden and pond; the Wellington Monument, a 220-ft-high obelisk commemorating the Irish-born general (see **Wellington**);

the Zoological Gardens (see **A–Z**); and the giant cross under which Pope John Paul II celebrated Mass during his visit in 1979. Also in the park are Aras an Uachtarain, the president's residence, first built in 1751 for the British Viceroy, and the American ambassador's residence, formerly the lodge of Britain's Chief Secretary. The park is relatively safe but you should take normal precautions, such as not leaving the main roads on your own or at night. See **PARKS & GARDENS**.

Police: The Garda (Garda Síochána) performs all the duties of a national police force. As in Britain, officers are unarmed in all but exceptional circumstances. One officer is a garda, more than one are gardai, pronounced 'gard-ee'. See **Crime & Theft**, **Emergency Numbers**.

Politics: Still dominated by the bloody Civil War of seven decades ago, when free staters supported the Treaty with Britain and republicans opposed what they saw as the betrayal of Ireland in the partitioning of the north. Fianna Fáil (meaning 'Soldiers of Destiny'), founded by republican Eamon de Valera (see **A–Z**) in 1926, has traditionally been the biggest party, supported by about half the electorate. Dublin accountant Charles Haughey has dominated the party as Taoiseach and opposition leader for more than a decade. Fine Gael (meaning 'Tribe of the Gaels') grew out of the old pro-Treaty faction and has alternated in power with Fianna Fáil since, under the leadership of Garret FitzGerald in the 1980s. The proportional-representation voting system means that most governments are coalitions, making the support of independent TDs and smaller parties like

Labour, the Progressive Democrats and the Workers' Party vital to gaining a majority. Irish politics can be abstruse but Fianna Fáil, Fine Gael and the Progressive Democrats are broadly mixed-economy Christian Democrats (Fianna Fáil being more right wing on social matters), Labour is like the British Labour Party, and the Workers' Party is soft Marxist. The presidency is a ceremonial post which the parties contest every seven years. It was won in 1990 by the independent candidate, Mary Robinson. See **Dáil Éireann**, **Ireland**.

Post Offices: The city's main post office is the GPO (see **WALK 1**, **A-Z**) in O'Connell St, where there are telephone, telex and fax facilities and a philatelic department (0800-2000 Mon.-Sat., 1030-1830 Sun.). Other post offices throughout the city are open 0900-1700 Mon.-Sat.

Prospect Cemetery: Also known as Glasnevin Cemetery and opened in 1832 on less than nine acres as a burial ground for Catholics, who were then second-class citizens. It has now grown to more than 100 acres. The outer wall still has the watchtowers originally erected to help guard against body snatchers. The biggest of the monuments is a 168-ft-high tower, completed in 1869, over the tomb of Daniel O'Connell (see **A-Z**), while one of the most striking is that at the grave of Charles Stewart Parnell (see **A-Z**). The cemetery is at Finglas Rd, next to the National Botanic Gardens (see **PARKS & GARDENS**), and is open daily.

Public Holidays: 1 Jan. (New Year's Day); 17 Mar. (St. Patrick's Day); Good Friday; Easter Monday; first Mon. in June; first Mon. in Aug.; last Mon. in Oct.; 25 Dec. (Christmas Day); 26 Dec. (St. Stephen's Day).

Pubs: There are more than 800 pubs in Dublin, ranging from spit-and-sawdust drinking halls to restored Victorian palaces. They are central to the city's cultural and social life, and all have the same purpose – a drink and a talk. Whether it's politics, the All-Ireland Hurling Final or tales of childhood in Co. Mayo, the crack is usually good. Children are allowed into many pubs during the day, while just reading the paper over a cup of tea or coffee is quite acceptable – you don't have to buy a drink, and most pubs now sell food. This, combined with a relaxed atmosphere, means women, singly or in groups, are a much more common sight than in pubs in Britain. The music scene also is geared around pubs, with places like O'Donoghue's renowned for traditional music and those like the Baggot Inn known as top rock venues. See PUBS, **Drinks**, **Licensing Laws**, **Music**.

Rabies: Ireland is rabies-free and on no account should you try to smuggle in an animal illegally. There are quarantine regulations for pets from outside the British Isles, and details can be obtained from your Irish consulate or embassy. Animals resident in the UK or Ireland for more than six months can move freely between the two countries.

Railways: Iarnród Éireann (Irish Rail) is part of CIE, the nationalized transport corporation and, like every national service, has both fans and critics, but the services are usually comfortable and reliable. Connolly Station, in the east of the city, serves north and west Ireland, while Heuston Station, near Phoenix Park, serves the south and southwest. Iarnród Éireann has super-standard and standard classes on its inter-city services (equivalent to first and second class). Rover-ticket combinations are good value, offering unlimited travel over 8- or 15-day periods, and are available for Iarnród Éireann alone, or in combination with Northern Ireland Railways or Bus Éireann (see **Buses**). Dublin Area Rapid Transport (DART) railway serves the Dublin Bay suburbs from Howth to Bray and has feeder services with Iarnród Éireann. See **DART**, **Transport**.

Religious Services:

Catholic – St. Mary's Pro-Cathedral, Marlborough St, tel: 745441.
Mass 1800 Sat., 1100 (Latin), 1230, 1630 (folk) Sun.

Anglican – St. Patrick's Cathedral, Patrick St, tel: 754817.
Holy Eucharist 0830, Matins 1115, Choral Evensong 1515 Sun.

Presbyterian – Abbey Presbyterian Church, Parnell Sq., tel: 742810.
1100, 1900 Sun.

Methodist – Dublin Central Mission, Lower Abbey St, tel: 742123.
1130 Sun.

Quaker – Eustace St. 1100 Sun.

Jewish (Orthodox) – Dublin Hebrew Congregation, 27 Adelaide Rd,
tel: 967351. Times vary on Fri., from 0915 Sat.

Jewish (Reform) – Dublin Jewish Progressive Congregation, 7 Leicester
Ave, tel: 907605. 2015 Fri., from 1030 Sat.

Muslim – Dublin Islamic Centre, 158 South Circular Rd, tel: 534858.
Juma prayers Fri., daily prayers.

Royal Dublin Society (RDS): Founded in 1731, the society spon-
sored the foundation of national institutions, including the Museum
(see MUSEUMS, A-Z), the Art Gallery (see ART GALLERIES), the Library (see
LIBRARIES) and the Botanic Gardens (see PARKS & GARDENS). The RDS
had several bases before moving to Leinster House (see A-Z) in 1815,
where it stayed until 1922, when the new Free State government expro-
priated the building for parliament. The RDS moved out to Ballsbridge,
where its 50-acre showgrounds had been bought in 1879. Its activities
now are confined to hosting events year-round, including the spring
Farming Show in May, the internationally rated Dublin Horse Show in
August (see **Events**) and various fairs, shows, concerts and society balls.

Sailing: Dun Laoghaire has four yacht clubs and Howth one, all catering mainly for larger boats and racing yachts, as well as motor cruisers. The clubs and both harbours offer good facilities for visiting yachtsmen. There are other, smaller clubs in Dublin Bay, most specializing in dinghy sailing. Yachts and dinghies can be brought into Ireland duty-free for short periods, while sea-going yachts must apply in advance to the harbour master of the port where they want to anchor. Bord Fáilte, the Irish Tourist Board (see **Tourist Information**), publishes an information leaflet (no. 28), and further information can be had from the Irish Yachting Association, 3 Park Rd, Dun Laoghaire, tel: 800239.

St. Patrick: A historical figure who is believed to have arrived in Ireland in AD 432. Legend says that he lit a huge fire on the Hill of Slane so that Ireland's High King might see it from his seat on the Hill of Tara and know that Christianity had arrived. Patrick established the Celtic church in Ireland and is believed to have come in AD 450 to Dublin, where he baptized people at a well. St. Patrick's Cathedral (see **CHURCHES**) was later built on the site and the well was marked by a memorial stone in the park alongside. St. Patrick's Day, 17 March, is celebrated in a large, colourful parade through Dublin (see **Events**).

St. Stephen's Green: Reputedly Europe's biggest city-centre park (22 acres), Stephen's Green, as it is known locally, has been a great place to rest from the pace of Dublin since 1663. The park is well laid out, with flower borders, gardens, walks, and a lake with waterfall and ducks. There are lunchtime concerts from the bandstand in summer. The arch at Grafton St is a memorial to the Royal Dublin Fusiliers who died in the Boer War (1899-1902). There are also sculptured tributes to Yeats (see **A-Z**) and Tone (see **A-Z**). See **PARKS & GARDENS, WALK 1**.

Shaw, George Bernard (1856-1950): Dublin-born Shaw moved in his early 20s to London where he made his name as a witty and cynical critic before embarking on a successful writing career. His works included *Man and Superman*, *Pygmalion* (basis for the musical and film *My Fair Lady*) and *St. Joan*. A noted socialist, he was one of the first to condemn Stalin's Russia. He was awarded the Nobel Prize in 1925.

Shopping: Dublin is a shopper's dream, with a wide variety of shops selling everything from designer fashion to Irish musical instruments and crafts. Grafton St, with its combination of old-style quality shops and modern boutiques, is the main shopping area, with the St. Stephen's Green Centre at one end. The other main shopping streets are O'Connell, Henry and Wicklow, all within easy walking distance of one another. Certain types of shops can be found in particular areas: books in Nassau St and on the south quays, antiques in Duke St and the Portobello area, crafts in Powerscourt Town House, and fashion in Grafton St. Many shops in the city centre stay open until 2000 on Thursdays and in the suburbs until 2100 on Thursdays and Fridays. Visitors from non-EC countries can reclaim VAT (Value Added Tax) under the Cashback scheme. Ask for Cashback vouchers when you buy goods (not services), then present them at the Cashback office at Dublin or Shannon airport when you leave Ireland – the money will be refunded or credited to your credit card account. See **SHOPPING**, **Best Buys**.

Smoking: The Irish are heavy smokers but new legislation means smoking is banned in public buildings such as banks, and on buses and DART trains. Many restaurants now have no-smoking tables but, unfortunately, most pubs have yet to discover the benefits of extractor fans.

Sports: Hurling and football, administered by the Gaelic Athletic Association (founded 1885), are Ireland's most popular sports, although Dublin city is a soccer and rugby stronghold. Croke Park is the Wembley of the GAA, where the All-Ireland cup finals are played every September, while Lansdowne Rd doubles for both rugby and soccer internationals. League rugby is played on Saturdays, and League of Ireland soccer games on Sundays. It is virtually impossible to get tickets for rugby internationals or All-Ireland games and, following the national team's 1990 World Cup success, soccer-international tickets are now sold for two games at a time, with prices around £30-60. All four games are widely played at amateur level on playing fields around the city. Tennis, golf and yachting are also popular, there is a packed summer road-racing schedule, and even league cricket is played. For tickets or further information, contact the following: GAA, Croke Park, tel: 363222; Football Association of Ireland, Merrion Sq., tel: 766864; Irish Rugby Football Union, Lansdowne Rd, tel: 684601. See **Fishing, Gaelic Games, Golf, Horse Riding & Trekking, Sailing, Tennis.**

Strongbow (c.1130-1176): The nickname of Richard de Clare, Earl of Pembroke, the 12thC Norman invader who was ally to Dermot, King of Leinster in his power battle with Rory O'Connor, High King Of Ireland. Strongbow was promised Dermot's daughter in marriage, as well as succession to the throne but he died without an heir to succeed him. The tomb of a knight in Christ Church Cathedral (see **CHURCHES, WALK 1**) is said to be his.

Swift, Jonathan (1667-1745): Dublin-born cleric and satirist best known as the author of *Gulliver's Travels*. In his early years, Swift railed privately about being stuck in 'wretched Dublin' and not being able to use his influence at court in London. He was savage in his writing against the British establishment on behalf of the rights of the Irish, particularly the poor of Dublin. To his fellow citizens he was best known as Dean of St. Patrick's Cathedral (1713-45) where he is buried (see **CHURCHES**). A deeply compassionate man, Swift left a bequest to found a home for the mentally ill. St. Patrick's Hospital in James St was duly established after his death and still cares for mentally ill patients.

Synge, John Millington (1871-1909): Died tragically young of cancer after displaying enormous though controversial talent as a playwright. His third play, *The Playboy of the Western World*, caused a riot at its first performances at the Abbey Theatre (see **THEATRES**) in 1907 for its mention of the word 'shift' (petticoat).

Taxis: Taxis in Dublin are relatively plentiful. They can be hired from ranks, hotels, railway and bus stations or hailed in the street. Fares are slightly more expensive than in the UK. The main city-centre ranks are at College Green, St. Stephen's Green and Aston Quay. Firms include the following: National Radio Cabs, tel: 772222 (24 hr); Co-Op Taxis, tel: 766666; Access, tel: 683333. See **Tipping**, **Transport**.

Telephones & Telegrams: Dublin's telecommunications are fast and efficient, although the rest of the country is still catching up with modern technology. Most calls are now STD and telex and fax services are available at the GPO (see **A-Z**) as well as at many hotels and business-service shops. Reduced rates apply 1800-0800 weekdays, at weekends and on public holidays. Calls dialled direct are slightly cheaper from private phones rather than from payphones.

Payphones are located at the GPO, in most pubs and on the streets, where they are of the open-hood style common in Britain and on the Continent. They take 10, 20 and 50p coins or international phone charge cards. There are still many old-style button A, button B phones in pubs and shops (insert the money before dialling, then press button A to be connected or button B to get your money back if there is no reply). Local calls cost 20p for the first five minutes, long-distance calls (over 50 miles) cost 45p for one minute (30p cheap rate).

To call Britain, dial 03 + city code + local number.

To dial all other countries, dial international-access code (16) + country code + area code + local number.

Country codes: Australia 61; Canada 1; New Zealand 64; USA 1.

There are five charge bands (public phone cheap rates per minute): EC countries 55p; rest of Europe and N. Africa £1.05; N. America £1; Far East £2.05; all other countries £2.90.

Operator services	10
Directory assistance (all Ireland)	190
Directory assistance (Britain)	197
International operator services	114

Television & Radio: State-owned Radio Telefís Éireann (RTE) runs two television channels. A third channel is planned to open in 1991-92. BBC, Channel 4 and ITV are universally available and many pubs, hotels and private homes also get Sky satellite channels on cable. RTE also runs two national radio stations (Radio 1 on 88.5 MHz, and 2 FM on 90.7 MHz) and there are a number of other national and local stations available in Dublin, mainly playing pop music on FM. BBC radio stations can also be picked up easily.

Tennis: There are many private and public courts – details from tourist information offices (see **A-Z**) or the Irish Lawn Tennis Association, 22 Upper Fitzwilliam St, tel: 610117. Public courts can be found at St. Anne's Park, Clontarf (see **PARKS & GARDENS**), Ellenfield Park, Whitehall, Bushy Park, Terenure, and Herbert Park, Ballsbridge.

Theatre: One of the continuing passions of Dublin life. The city has produced playwrights from Sheridan and Wilde (see **A-Z**) to O'Casey (see **A-Z**) and Beckett (see **A-Z**) but the founding of the Abbey Theatre (see **Yeats**) launched the modern theatre movement. There is a thriving amateur and semi-professional fringe theatre performing at any of the numerous small and large venues. Actors such as Milo O'Shea, the late Ray MacInally and Donal McCann have made international reputations while treading the boards in Dublin. See **THEATRES**.

Time Difference: There is no difference with the UK, as Ireland follows GMT and BST. Eastern Standard Time is five hours behind.

Tipping: Service charge is included on many hotel and restaurant bills; otherwise, tip 10% if the service merits it. Tip pub waitresses 30-50p, depending on the size of the order, and hotel porters 50p per bag. Taxi drivers get 10-15%, but remember that any tip is purely optional.

Toilets: Public toilets are few and far between, and everyone uses those in shops, pubs and hotels, few of which object. In Gaelic, 'mna' means 'women' and 'fir' means 'men'.

Tone, Wolfe (1763-98): The Dublin-born Protestant leader of the United Irishmen who tried to achieve an independent Irish republic based on the ideals of the French Revolution. A sporadic and haphazard insurrection was suppressed after two years when a French force was defeated in August 1798. Tone was sentenced to death but died in prison, probably by his own hand.

Tourist Information: Bord Fáilte, the Irish Tourist Board, publishes an extensive range of general and specialist brochures and operates tourist information offices (TIOs) at home and abroad. The Dublin & East TIO has a large and knowledgeable staff at 14 Upper O'Connell St, tel: 747733, and can help with bookings of accommodation and tours throughout Ireland. There are smaller offices at the airport, tel: 376387; St. Michael's Wharf, Dun Laoghaire, tel: 806984; and in Bray (June-Sep. only), tel: 867128. See **Accommodation**, **Tours**, **Walks**, **What's On**.

Tours: Guided walking tours have long been a popular way of seeing the city. Most last about two hours and cost £2-3.50. They are advertised in the press (see **Newspapers**, **What's On**) and at tourist information offices (see **A–Z**). Among the best are the following:

Historical Walking Tours – hosted by history graduates of Trinity College; starts at the front gates of the college, daily 1100, 1300, 1500.

Old Dublin Tours – meet at main gate of Christ Church Cathedral (see **CHURCHES**) 1030, 1400 Fri., 1030 Sat., 1400 Sun.

Dublin Footsteps – literary, medieval or Georgian walks; meet inside Bewley's Café, Grafton St, 1030, 1430 Mon.-Sat., 1100, 1500 Sun.

Dublin Literary Pub Crawl (summer only) – combines beer and literary history; starts at the Bailey (see **PUBS 3**), Duke St, 1930 Tue.-Thu.

Dublin Walks – with Éamonn MacThomáis, through the Liberties (Sat.) or Literary and Georgian Dublin (Sun.); starts at Molly Malone statue,

Grafton St, 1400.

Dublin Bus runs tours of the city, and to the north and south coast (all year; daily in summer). £6, child £3, departing from outside Dublin Bus office, 59 Upper O'Connell St, tel: 734222.

Transport: Dublin is a fairly compact city and is easy to get around on efficient public transport: buses, Iarnrod Éireann and the DART railways. The main drawbacks are that most bus routes cover either the north or south sides, so cross-city journeys usually mean two buses, while the DART runs only around Dublin Bay in the east. Dublin is well connected with the USA, Britain and the rest of the EC by air and there are good ferry routes to Britain and France. See **Airport**, **Bicycle & Motorcycle Hire**, **Buses**, **Car Hire**, **Driving**, **Ferries**, **Railways**, **Taxis**.

Trinity College (TCD): The only college in Dublin University, founded in 1592 by Elizabeth I to consolidate the Reformation, it remained a bulwark of Protestantism in Ireland for four centuries. The restriction on Catholics was dropped in 1873 but the Catholic Church maintained until 1970 its own ban on its members being students. The 18th and 19thC buildings, grounds and courtyards on the 40-acre site (which includes a cricket ground) are an architectural delight. There are about 7000 full-time students at TCD, with hundreds of foreign language students taking their places during the summer vacation. Former Trinity students include Oliver Goldsmith and Oscar Wilde (see **A-Z**). See **BUILDINGS**, **LIBRARIES**, **Trinity College Library**.

Trinity College Library: The state's biggest library, Trinity is entitled under the Copyright Act to receive a copy of every book published in Britain and Ireland, and its seven libraries (not all on the main site) contain almost three million volumes. The impressive Long Room has many treasures among its manuscripts and bound volumes, including the Book of Kells (see **A-Z**), the Book of Durrow (7thC), the Book of Dimma (8thC) and the Book of Armagh (9thC) which contains the New Testament as well as the life and confessions of St. Patrick (see **A-Z**). The library is administered from the Berkeley Library, a 1960s building named after Bishop George Berkeley, after whom a town, and campus of the University of California are also named. See **LIBRARIES**.

Ulysses: See **Bloomsday**, **Joyce**.

University College Dublin (UCD): The Dublin college of the national University of Ireland (the others are in Cork, Galway and Limerick). The University of Ireland was founded in 1853 as a Catholic university by Anglican convert Cardinal John Henry Newman in buildings on the south side of St. Stephen's Green (the Byzantine-style University Church is still there). UCD now has an extensive modern campus in the south-side suburb of Belfield, near Donnybrook.

Vikings: Dublin started developing as a major town only after Norse raiders found the shelter of its bay around AD 840. The Vikings landed to find a cluster of Gaelic monastic settlements at a ford where the Dodder River joins the Liffey and they built a stronghold (see **Wood Quay**) but it was only with the arrival of Danish forces 12 years later that they began to prosper. Irish and Vikings fought repeatedly over the years but there was a steady mingling of cultures, epitomized by Danish King Sitric's conversion to Christianity in AD 925. The Vikings brought great wealth from their raids, as well as skills such as weaving, tanning and shipbuilding. Their influence waned after the Anglo-Norman forces of Strongbow (see **A-Z**) conquered Dublin in 1170 and set up a new order. See **Ireland**.

Walks: Dublin is a compact city best discovered on foot. Phoenix Park (see **PARKS & GARDENS**, **A-Z**) and St. Anne's Park (see **PARKS & GAR-DENS**) are great for a stroll, winter or summer, while Dubliners are fond of stepping out along the restored Grand Canal (see **Canals**) from Baggot St to Charlemont St Bridge. Howth (see **WALK 2**) and Dalkey are also popular: Dun Laoghaire tourist information office, St. Michael's Wharf, tel: 806984, has pamphlet guides for walks in the Dun Laoghaire/Dalkey/Killiney area (see **EXCURSION 1**). Serious hillwalkers can tackle the 78-mile Wicklow Way, through the scenic mountains south of Dublin, while the less ambitious can opt for smaller sections of the marked route. Bord Fáilte, the Irish Tourist Board (see **Tourist Information**), produces information sheets on the Wicklow Way, and there is a mass of guidebooks in the shops. See **WALKS**, **Tours**.

Wellington, Duke of (1769-1852): Arthur Wellesley, born at Mornington House, Merrion Sq., was the hero who defeated Napoleon at Waterloo in 1815. The Iron Duke later became Britain's only Irish-born prime minister (1828-30), at the time of the granting of Catholic Emancipation. He played down his Dublin origins but the city did not forget him, raising one of the world's tallest obelisks in his honour (see **Phoenix Park**). The battle scenes around its pedestal were cast from captured cannon.

What's On: There is a good range of listings magazines, the best of which are *In Dublin* and *Hot Press* (music). Daily newspapers also have good what's-on sections, the *Irish Times* carrying a comprehensive guide to the more formal art, classical music and lecture circuits. Billboards and leaflets from tourist information offices (see **A-Z**) and hotels are also good guides. See **Events**, **Newspapers**.

Whiskey: Irish whiskey – the word comes from the Gaelic *uisce beat-hadh*, meaning 'water of life' – is distinguished from Scotch by being distilled three times rather than twice, giving a smoother, more mellow taste. Pub measures are larger than those in Britain. Whiskey, usually taken just with water, is often a chaser accompaniment to a pint of stout. Power's is the biggest-selling brand. See **Drinks**, **Pubs**.

Wilde, Oscar (1854-1900): Educated at Trinity College (see **A-Z**) and Oxford University, he moved in 1879 to London, where his wit and talent led to a string of theatrical successes, including *The Importance of Being Earnest* and *Lady Windermere's Fan*, and the novel *The Picture of Dorian Gray*. Prosecution for his homosexual activities led to public humiliation, imprisonment and his early death in poverty in France.

Wood Quay: Site of the extensive remains of Viking (see **A-Z**) and medieval Dublin which were unearthed during preparatory work for the building of Dublin corporation offices. Despite massive protests, the corporation went ahead with the building of the monstrous concrete block which now scars the area around Christ Church Cathedral. This

incident was the worst example of the corporation-approved planning blight which saw the destruction of much of old Dublin up to the mid-1980s.

Writers: See **Literary Dublin**.

Yeats, William Butler (1865-1939):
Born to an Anglo-Irish family from Co. Sligo and educated in Dublin, Yeats had a love-hate relationship with the city. In 1898, with Lady Augusta Gregory and Edward Martin, he started the Irish Literary Theatre which later became the Abbey Theatre (see **THEATRES**). His own plays, including *Cathleen ni Houlihan*, were presented there and he strongly supported Synge (see **A-Z**) and O'Casey (see **A-Z**), going on stage to lambast audiences who rioted during performances of their plays. A Nobel Prize winner in 1923, he was a Senator from 1922-28 and is commemorated in a sculpture by Henry Moore in St. Stephen's Green (see **PARKS & GARDENS**, **A-Z**).

Youth Hostels: An Oige, the Irish Youth Hostel Association, 39 Mountjoy Sq., tel: 364749, is part of the international organization and can give details of membership and facilities. It runs a hostel at 61 Mountjoy Sq., tel: 301766 (from £6.50 per night, including breakfast). YWCA is at 64 Baggot St, tel: 608452 (£7 a night, including breakfast).

Zoological Gardens: The world's third-oldest public zoo was founded in Phoenix Park (see **PARKS & GARDENS**, **A-Z**) in 1830 but has been under constant threat of closure for financial reasons in recent years. It has had particular success in raising lions and supplying other zoos worldwide. An appealing feature is that most of its wide collection of tropical animals is kept in bar-free enclosures. A variety of waterfowl inhabits the natural lake, while in the Children's Corner there is a collection of domestic animals which youngsters can meet. The zoo has a restaurant, shops and gardens. 0930-1800 Mon.-Sat., 1100-1700 Sun. £3.30, child £1.60, family ticket £10.50. Tel: 771425.

National Botanic Gardens